CREATIVE METHODS IN
ORGANIZATIONAL RESEARCH

CREATIVE METHODS IN
ORGANIZATIONAL RESEARCH

MIKE BROUSSINE

with

Mick Beeby, Robert French, Louise Grisoni, Philip Kirk,
Margaret Page and Peter Simpson

Los Angeles • London • New Delhi • Singapore

First published 2008

SAGE Publications Ltd
1 Oliver's Yard
55 City Road
London EC1Y 1SP

SAGE Publications Inc.
2455 Teller Road
Thousand Oaks, California 91320

SAGE Publications India Pvt Ltd
B 1/I 1 Mohan Cooperative Industrial Area
Mathura Road
New Delhi 110 044

SAGE Publications Asia-Pacific Pte Ltd
33 Pekin Street #02-01
Far East Square
Singapore 048763

Library of Congress Control Number: 2007933077

British Library Cataloguing in Publication data

A catalogue record for this book is available from
the British Library

ISBN 978-1-4129-0133-8
ISBN 978-1-4129-0134-5 (pbk)

Typeset by CEPHA Imaging Pvt. Ltd., Bangalore, India
Printed in Great Britain by TJ International Ltd., Padstow, Cornwall
Printed on paper from sustainable resources

CONTENTS

CONTRIBUTORS AND AUTHORS

Mick Beeby has a Masters in Organisation Studies from Leeds University, and is a Fellow of the Higher Education Academy. Mick has built a successful academic track-record in teaching, research and consultancy over a 35-year career at Bristol Business School, University of the West of England (UWE). Mick has been consistently active in research, using a range of creative methodologies – including action, experimental and collaborative research designs – to inquire into areas of professional interest. These have included leadership, dialogue, organisational learning and the gendered nature of sense-making. Mick has published in leading UK management journals, and has presented his research at national and international management conferences.

Mike Broussine was Director of the Research Unit for Organisation Studies at Bristol Business School (BBS) up to 2006, and his main research interests include emotions and the politics of organisations; public services leadership; gender and diversity; and organisational research methods. Until 2007 he was Joint Programme Director of UWE's MSc Leadership and Organisation of Public Services, a programme designed to promote leadership development and learning across the public, private and voluntary sectors. Mike has written extensively about aspects of public services leadership, and has published critical reflections of the processes of organisational facilitation and consultancy. He offers consultancy, action research, action learning and leadership development in client organisations. Mike is a Visiting Research Fellow at BBS.

Dr Robert French is Reader in Organisation Studies at Bristol Business School, UWE, and also works as an independent organisational consultant. He has a particular interest in issues of teaching and learning; in leadership; in the experience of role in organisations; and in the application of psychoanalysis in group and organisational contexts. He has written widely in these areas, and he recently edited the papers of David Armstrong (*Organization in the Mind*, Karnac, 2005), and has co-edited two books, *Rethinking Management Education* (Sage Publications, 1996, with Chris Grey), and *Group Relations, Management, and Organization* (Oxford University Press, 1999, with Russ Vince).

Dr Louise Grisoni has been Head of the School of Organization Studies for six years and Director of Learning, Teaching and Assessment at BBS in 2006–2007. Her teaching interests include organisational analysis and behaviour, and organisational learning and leadership. Her research interests include group and inter-group dynamics, leadership and gender, experiential learning and creative research methods. She has presented regularly at conferences nationally and internationally (including the European Group for Organisation Studies – EGOS, and the Art of Management Conference). Working with poetry as a creative research method has become a principal focus for her work. She has developed a way of using poetic forms such as haiku and *"corps exquis"* to access implicit organisational knowledge. She has also used poetry as a reflective tool for making sense of personal organisational experience.

Philip Kirk has spent nearly 35 years in higher education, previously working for two years in the NHS and for five years with Cadbury Schweppes. Phil has an enduring belief in the potential of education to produce beneficial social change in the contexts of people's lives, individually and collectively. To this end, developing critical consciousness, a spirit of inquiry and mobilising agency have been important educational objectives. Born in India, Phil has an international perspective, and a passion for Africa has seen him visit the continent on numerous occasions. Phil's last role before retiring from full-time education in 2007 was Head of the School of Organisation Studies at Bristol Business School. He is a Visiting Research Fellow at BBS.

Dr Margaret Page joined BBS as a Senior Lecturer in Organisation Studies in 2005. She is Joint Programme Director for UWE's MSc Leadership and Organisation of Public Services, and teaches in modules leading and managing change on post-graduate and undergraduate programmes. Her current research concerns inquiry-based methodologies for leadership, learning and change in organisations, and the challenges of sustaining effective collaborative working across organisational boundaries. Margaret draws from psychodynamic and systemic perspectives for understanding the dynamics of learning and resistance to change in specific organisational, business and social contexts. She has been an action-learning set facilitator, facilitating partnership working within adult and children's services in health and social care.

Dr Peter Simpson is Reader in Organization Studies and Director of Business Development at Bristol Business School. He has published on strategic and cultural leadership, organisational and management roles, and the place of "not knowing" in leadership and management practice. He has used "storytelling" as a research method in all of these contexts. His current interests are in the application of complex systems theory and psychoanalytical theory to the study of organisations.

He lectures in organisational leadership, learning and change to undergraduate and post-graduate audiences. Recent consultancy and research contracts have involved working with middle and senior management teams on the leadership of strategic and cultural change initiatives and processes of learning in the face of uncertainty.

INTRODUCTION

while they are perusing this book, they [readers] *should ask themselves if it contains a natural delineation of human passions, human characters, and human incidents; and if the answer be favourable to the author's wishes, that they should consent to be pleased in spite of that most dreadful enemy to our pleasures, our own pre-established codes of decision.*

William Wordsworth and Samuel Taylor Coleridge, *Lyrical Ballads* (Bristol, 1798) from the *'Avertisement'*[sic] (preface)

Recent developments in the theory and practice of qualitative organizational and management research have opened up opportunities and the hope that researchers can employ a greater range of creative methodologies and methods that enable further and deeper understanding about human experience in social systems. Thus, researchers may from time to time be open to the surprise that, for example, eighteenth-century Romantic poets have something relevant to say to us across the years – to remind us perhaps that our fascination with learning more about 'human passions, human characters, and human incidents' is an enduring facet of our being. The aim of this book is to explore how poetry, the visual arts, drama and stories can offer us avenues through which we may understand more about the rich and complex human experience in organizations.

Research in organizations can often feel like a privileged experience: people will tell the organizational or management researcher things that they might not otherwise have the opportunity to say. An enjoyable aspect of our jobs as academics is to observe the growth in academic and research capacity in our students. Students often report getting a 'buzz' out of doing research. They learn more about research methodologies and what it takes to inquire into aspects of social systems and complex human experience. They also report that they learn much more about themselves.

This is not to say that organizational research is unproblematic. It is highly challenging as well as enlightening, and we share some of these challenges in this book. One of the epistemological challenges that we address in Chapter 1, is the worry sometimes that research can be seen as something that is 'done to people'. Such a notion perpetuates the myth that research is not relevant to the real problems and challenges that people face in organizations, and researchers who go into organizations with their tape recorders and questionnaires can be seen as a distraction from the real work that people have to get on with. Indeed, it is a common experience for many managers to be overwhelmed by the numbers of questionnaires that come across their desks. We ourselves have been culprits in adding to a sense of 'questionnaire fatigue' in some of the organizations that we have worked with.

Our interest in developing this book is to contribute to, and to help the researcher make sense of, an emerging and developing tradition among organizational and management researchers who are committed to using creative methods to understand more about people's experiences of organizational life. We seek to achieve this both through critical reflections on our own research practices, and by bringing together the reflections and experiences of researchers who have used such methods in their organizational research. There is of course a huge range of potential research approaches that could be adopted, but our purpose is to argue that creative forms of inquiry, set within a collaborative approach, can make a significant contribution to our repertoire of qualitative and interpretive methodologies. Inevitably we are writing this book from our own experiences – our successes and mistakes. Our intention is, along the way, to communicate the debt that we owe to a range of colleagues in academia and elsewhere who began the journey towards creative methodologies before us. We aim also to make an enthusiastic case for creative research approaches, but at the same time to encourage the development of a reflexive and critical stance about them. The book represents a significant part of our own journeys of learning and challenge about what it is to be a creative organizational and management researcher.

As we have said, the use of creative approaches in organizational research is growing, and to some extent we are writing this book in order to take stock of, and enable practical access to, these methods. The book takes up the challenge set out in a literature about creative and metaphor-based qualitative inquiry (e.g. Fineman, 2000; Finley, 2003; Mullen, 2003; Watkins, 2006) to focus discussion of methodologies on practice, i.e. on actually doing research. Fineman (2000) suggested that we can learn from the poet, novelist and dramatist, and that research does not lose its rigour by 'finding different voices, or expressive forms, to convey crucial experiences and meanings' (Fineman, 2000, p. 15). Mullen, in introducing a special edition of *Qualitative Inquiry*, talked of 'an explosion' (Mullen, 2003, p. 165) that has occurred recently in arts-based inquiry in the social sciences. This experimentation, she suggested, took social researchers 'beyond scientific modes of discourse', and it underscored, among other matters, the need for political agency for 'the voices of those who are not heard'. Watkins (2006) similarly argues that there have been a number of challenges to the hegemonic status of 'scientific research' recently (Watkins, 2006, p. 3), including a growth in the contributions that the humanities and the field of social inquiry can make to management and organizational research. In a special issue of *Organization Studies*, Schreyögg and Höpfl (2004) suggested that the idea of 'theatre' could be used as a vehicle for organizational inquiry to provide fresh insights into organizational dynamics, both by looking at *organizations as theatres*, and by looking at *theatre in organizations*. Kusenbach (2005) reported on the proceedings of a conference, *The State of the Art of Qualitative Social Research in Europe*, held in Berlin in 2004. She reviewed a range of research methodological trends, discussing the growing diversity of research tools and designs. She reported how a number of presenters at this conference had noticed significant increases in the use of visual research methods and data sets, and in experimental methods that recreate real-life situations with subjects. As just one example, Kusenbach (2005) cited the work of Shalva Weil (Israel), who employed a creative research method – the use of maps drawn by Israeli children of their schools, in combination with interviews – which brought to the foreground her subjects' perceptions and emotions, which would not, it was argued, surface otherwise. At the same conference, David Silverman (UK) suggested that qualitative researchers need to inquire into the construction of meaning within the multiple contexts of social reality, one of which is the collaborative production of narrative accounts.

The authors contributing to this text have had some part to play in the development of this emergent approach, and share their learning, experiences and approaches with respect to the use of creative methods in organizational and management research. Mick Beeby (Chapter 3) has employed a creative approach to dialogue, and suggests that dialogue enables people who are trying to work together, like researchers and co-researchers, to reveal, encounter and capture the nature, origins and consequences of sense-making processes in the 'here and now' of human interactions in organizations (Beeby *et al.*, 2002). Mike Broussine (Chapter 4) has used art and drawings in organizational research for some time – in particular to explore organizational members' feelings about organizational change – and argues that such methods can provide an immediacy of expression of feelings from the emotions that may be captured or evoked through visual metaphors; and from the fact that drawings may give us insight into unconscious as well as conscious thoughts and feelings (Broussine and Vince, 1995; Vince and Broussine, 1996). Peter Simpson (Chapter 5) has employed the method of eliciting participants' stories about their experiences in a series of inquiries into facets of organizational leadership, and comes from a position that stories are central to processes of sense-making within organizations. Peter has worked closely with Robert French (Chapter 7) in this endeavour (Simpson *et al.*, 2002; French and Simpson, 2006). Louise Grisoni (Chapter 6) has experimented with the use of poetry as a reflective and analytical tool of inquiry that, she argues, can access tacit knowledge, inner thoughts and feelings (Grisoni and Kirk, 2006). In this way, poetry is used for personal reflection to deal with complexity and an analysis of previously unprocessed data, and she shows how a group of research participants may create collective, collaborative poems that help to develop new understandings of a research question. Louise was (with Per Darmer) a convenor for the Poetry and Organizing stream at the third *Art of Management and Organisation Conference* held in Krakow, Poland, in September 2006. Philip Kirk and Robert French (Chapter 7) make a case for methods of inquiry based in theatre and masks, i.e. that these can allow both researcher and research participants to gain access to their experiences and explore their actions, thoughts and feelings, in different and creative ways, with the possibility of new insights and understandings. They show how masks and theatre can make it possible for people to engage in the inquiry in active, imaginative and intuitive ways as they use metaphors to describe events and seek explanations (Kirk, 2003).

We may detect from the foregoing brief review of writing and experiences, both the potential power and the contribution of creative methods in organizational research. We may notice that a set of principles about their use has emerged. Firstly, advocates and practitioners give emphasis to enabling the expression of voice, in order to engage research participants who might otherwise be silenced or marginalized. The intention for many researchers in this emerging tradition is not just to enable participants to find their agency. The assumption for many is that creative approaches may generate empirical material that offers in-depth understanding of experience of social systems that might not surface otherwise. The aim is to understand more about the affective domain in organizational life, whether directly communicated in creative encounters with organizational researchers, or more indirectly through metaphorical and/or symbolic material. This depth includes possibilities of accessing tacit, unstated, unacknowledged and unconscious material. Secondly, researchers who are interested in learning more about people's experiences through creative methods assume that the researcher/research subject relationship is an active, participative and collaborative one. The implication is that the effective use of creative methods requires a reflexive awareness on the part of researchers about nature of their power relationships with participants. We may see from our brief review here that these researchers implicitly and sometimes explicitly reject a positivist notion of 'doing research' on people.

These two principles – the enabling of the expression of voice, and a participative and collaborative relationship – begin to construct the philosophical scaffolding for this book. The first two chapters discuss these principles in more depth, and provide a theoretical framing or container for the range of methods that are explored in the subsequent chapters.

WHAT THE BOOK IS ABOUT AND WHO IT IS FOR

The central concern of this book is with enabling people to express their feelings, recollections and reflections of organizational experience when it may be difficult to do so in other circumstances or by attempting to use other methodologies. 'Creative' approaches are those which utilize inventive and imaginative modes of data collection, and which encourage and enable research participants to access and express a rich and multifaceted account of their lived experiences. Such data are not merely constituted of rational or analytical empirical material, but as importantly they include the emotional, unconscious, political, processual and social texture of organizational life.

This book is primarily a 'how to' text for the organization or management researcher, bringing together a range of creative methods set within an overarching intention to work collaboratively with research participants and organizations. The reader therefore might be a student who is about to undertake a study leading to the writing of a dissertation or doctoral thesis; alternatively, she or he might be an experienced researcher who is interested in extending his or her repertoire of qualitative methods in the context of organizationally based inquiry. We hope also that this text will add to the resources available to those whose responsibilities include the supervision of students and others who wish to adopt creative approaches in their research.

In writing and organizing this book, we have assumed that the reader has a reasonable knowledge about the nature of qualitative research and associated methodologies. Similarly, we assume that she or he is conversant with some of the debates concerning research paradigms. In saying this, we are by no means minimizing the need for researchers to address the paradigmic underpinnings of their research: as Easterby-Smith *et al.* (2004, p. 27) put it:

> Failure to think through philosophical issues … , while not necessarily fatal, can seriously affect the quality of management research, and they are central to the notion of research design.

Therefore, while we make no attempt to provide a comprehensive discussion about research philosophies and paradigms in general terms (the reader is recommended to consult Chapter 3 of Easterby-Smith *et al.*, 2004), our first two chapters set out the main assumptions that we believe offer the conditions for the effective use of creative methods in organizational research. The aim is that, having consulted this text; attempted some of the discussion questions that may be found at the end of each chapter; and taken up some of the recommended reading and references, the researcher will feel sufficiently confident to undertake (perhaps with supervision) a study using one or more of the creative approaches discussed. Very importantly, the researcher will be able to do this while holding a critical self- and methodological awareness based on the strengths and weaknesses of the chosen method or methods. We also include a number of case studies – stories – that report the experiences of a range of organizational and management researchers. Our hope is that they will illustrate the arguments being proposed, because invariably they hold an eloquence that comes from the researcher's reflection on a significant experience.

ORGANIZATION OF THE BOOK

The creative approaches that we deal with are:

- Creative dialogue (Chapter 3)
- Drawings and art (Chapter 4)

- Stories (Chapter 5)
- Poetry (Chapter 6)
- Theatre and masks (Chapter 7)

Chapter 1: *Underlying Theory and Principles*. Before we get into the approaches themselves, this chapter sets the methods within the context of contemporary theory and practice in qualitative inquiry. It therefore discusses the theoretical basis for the methods explored in subsequent chapters by examining some of the challenges of researching social phenomena in organizations, including giving attention to the rich and multifaceted dimensions of human experience. We argue that, at the basis of creative research methods, lies an aim to enable different expressive forms to be appreciated as a way of understanding more about organizational life, and that the study of organizations may be enriched by seeing what other branches of human endeavour, including the arts, have to offer the researcher.

Chapter 2: *The Seductive Qualities of Creative Methods: Critical Awareness* – continues the process of setting out the theoretical and philosophical basis for creative methods, but now concentrating on the possible motivations and awareness required on the part of the creative researcher. We begin by emphasizing the fact that creative approaches can be seductive, which is both their potential strength and their weakness, and it is here that we argue that their use requires a critical self-awareness on the part of the researcher. In particular, we argue for the need to give attention to the ethical and methodological challenges of working with research participants' feelings and personal experiences as 'data'.

Chapters 3 to 7 deal in depth with each of the creative methods. These chapters are structured so that the reader may focus on those aspects that meet his or her needs. The early sections introduce the approach, providing a summary of relevant principles and theoretical underpinnings that are specific to the method itself, with an exploration of the origins of the method. The heart of each chapter then explains how the method can be used in the field; the nature of the data that are generated; and examples of how such data can be analysed. In summary, each chapter will include these common elements:

- What this approach is, and why it should be used
- Underlying principles and theory
- How to use the approach
- Case studies of where the approach has been used before
- Working with the data
- Conclusion
- Further reading
- Discussion questions

Chapter 3: *Creative Dialogue*. Dialogue is a process of collaborative organizational inquiry. It can surface and contribute to the formation of collective meanings that frequently remain unrealized in groups. Taking us beyond a focus-group approach, dialogue as research allows new meanings to unfold as collective 'thinking out loud' occurs. As well as being a form of action research, dialogic methods can give the researcher access to subtle and hidden aspects of research participants' subjective experience as they engage with organizational tasks and processes of organizing. As well as describing how dialogue may be used creatively in inquiry, this early chapter sets out some further important principles that underpin the research approaches that we cover.

Chapter 4: *Drawings and Art*. The process of producing art and drawings can be a spontaneous, direct and rich experience for research participants. We will show how drawings and art can be used to access a person's and a group's unconscious feelings – a function which is supported by literature in the art therapy field. This approach is underpinned by a belief that it allows research participants to give voice to feelings and experience that may otherwise be hard to put into words.

Chapter 5: *Stories*. Stories are central to processes of sense-making and identity development within organizations. As a natural part of organizational life, individuals work with and communicate their experiences by telling. This chapter outlines methods that elicit stories to provide the researcher with access to rich data from the 'middle ground' between culturally formed discourse and the raw reality of participants' lived experience.

Chapter 6: *Poetry*. Wordsworth described poetry as 'the spontaneous overflow of powerful feelings; it takes its origin from emotion recollected in tranquillity'. Working with poetry in research can help to capture aspects of organizational members' experiences that are deep and significant. For example, the co-creation of poetic forms may reveal underlying emotions, meanings and assumptions that more traditional textual forms may fail to reach.

Chapter 7: *Masks and Theatre*. The imagery of theatre and masks offers an alternative approach for identifying and making sense of the unfolding dramas of organizational life. The histories, comedies, tragedies and variety of roles that make up organizational dramas are used as a method of inquiry to allow the researcher to gain access to the depth of feelings that people experience in organizations.

Chapter 8: *Reflections*. The final chapter offers critical reflections about what we have learned about creative methods for management and organizational research. The chapter addresses key questions about the legitimacy and validity of the methods, and suggests how we can defend our methodological choices. Chapter 8 suggests that creative methods enable us to access different ways of knowing, and the concept of 'congruence' between them is offered as a basis for research validity.

UNDERPINNINGS

CHAPTER 1

UNDERLYING THEORY AND PRINCIPLES

Mike Broussine

OVERVIEW

- **How a creative capacity for expression may offer ways of inquiring into human experience in organizations**
- **The challenges involved in researching social phenomena in organizations**
- **Working with multifaceted dimensions of human experience**
- **How creative methods can make it possible to find different expressive forms**
- **The use of metaphor in organizational and management research**
- **The importance of a collaborative researcher/ research participant relationship in the use of creative methods**
- **Conclusion**
- **Discussion questions**
- **Further reading**

Take a moment to look at Figure 1.1, showing a painting by the Norwegian artist Edvard Munch (1863–1944). This iconic expressionist work is regarded as an emblem of alienation in a modern age. For our purposes, it is instructive to understand something of the emotions that provoked the artist to produce this painting.

Figure 1.1 *The Scream* by Edvard Munch (1893) © Munch Museum/Munch–Ellingsen Group, BONO, Oslo/DACS, London 2007

Munch wrote:

> I was walking along a path with two friends – the sun was setting – suddenly the sky turned blood red. I paused, feeling exhausted, and leaned on the fence – there was blood and tongues of fire above the blue-black fjord and the city. My friends walked on, and I stood there trembling with anxiety – and I sensed an infinite scream passing through nature.

One way of beginning to understand the potential of creative research methods might be for the researcher to visit an art gallery, read a piece of poetry, read a fairy-tale, take in a film or go to the theatre. We invite the reader to take a moment to recollect any feelings that a particular painting, story, film, play or poem evoked in you. For example, when you look at Edvard Munch's painting, or a painting by Jackson Pollock, read Franz Kafka's *The Trial* or Rupert Brooke's wartime sonnets *1914* ('If I should die, think only this of me …'), what emotions are stirred? What experiences are recollected? We know of a college principal who will sometimes visit a gallery and will wander the halls and corridors until a picture somehow demands her attention. She will then sit or stand before the painting, allowing it to have its impact upon her. In this way, she says, she inquires into deeper realms of her own thoughts, emotions and experience. Sometimes these encounters with art help directly with issues in her work.

When we are touched in any way by a painting, play, film, poem, story or piece of music, then we know that the creative arts have a power to provoke and evoke feelings. Isadora Duncan is reputed to have said, 'If I could say it in words, I wouldn't need to dance', and the inter-war American artist Edward Hopper commented, similarly: 'If I could say it in words there would be no reason to paint'. The arts have always been intimately connected with the feelings that they arouse. Paul Cezanne said, 'A work of art which did not begin in emotion is not art', and Aristotle asserted that, 'The aim of art is to represent not the outward appearance of things, but their inward significance'.

Creativity, whether in painting, drama, poetry or story, may be seen as an expression of the artist's inner self, which may then touch the inner self of the audience. In essence, the purpose of this book is to show how this capacity for expression of the self may offer ways of inquiring into human experience in organizations.

The first of our case study stories is provided by Sue Congram, who is a PhD student. Her study's working title is 'A Jungian-based investigation into changing patterns of leadership in business', and she tells us her story about how and why art and creativity became important in her research.

A PhD student's story – Sue

I have used art and poetry to inform and excite my PhD research from the point of application right through to today – now three years into a six-year part-time study. Not only does art maintain a balance for me in a world of logic and scientific rigour, it also enables me to maintain my authenticity.

> … And I have felt
> a presence that disturbs me with the joy
> of elevated thought; a sense sublime
> of something far more deeply interfused,
> whose dwelling is the light of setting suns,
> and the round ocean and the living air,
> and the blue sky, and in the mind of man;

Continued

a motion and a spirit, that impels
all thinking things, all objects of thought,
And rolls through all things ...

William Wordsworth

As I approached my application process for my PhD, I came across this poem – it captured the essence of where I was at that time, and still speaks to me now. At times when I feel stuck, overly challenged or weighted down with reading and writing, I come back to this poem. This poem is the first writing in my journal, which I started early in my studies. It is a PhD journal that is probably quite different to conventional PhD journals. I keep track of thoughts, images, words, poems and questions that leap out at me when studying particular themes. If I am stuck with a question, then I doodle, write, draw or paint the question, either in my journal, or separately. I am a keen photographer, and sometimes images connect with questions and ideas.

Art and creative processes provide us with metaphors and symbols, a language of the not yet known. They live through a part of us that is not thought. I cannot imagine doing a PhD without exercising this creative, artistic and intuitive part of me. It is a rich feeding ground that informs my writing, my thinking and my ideas, and helps keep me going when the journey gets tough.

THE NATURE OF RESEARCHING SOCIAL PHENOMENA IN ORGANIZATIONS

Research is the attempt to explore and explain. The belief that the world is amenable to understanding supports our endeavours, and this belief is particularly important when explanation is elusive. There are times when not only are others unconvinced by our arguments, but we fail even to convince ourselves that our studies have any merit. At times like this, it is only the belief that there is value in the search, and some possibility of success, that sustains us. At the heart of the research mentality is a persistence that will help us to pursue the exploration, even in the face of phenomena that do not wish to reveal their secrets.

The scientific and positivist perspective has been applied in many areas with determination, and has explained aspects of the physical world that were previously a mystery. These discoveries have provided the basis for a civilization that has a greater capacity for wealth creation than any the world has ever known. As a consequence of scientific research, we can produce food efficiently and in great volume, we can administer health care to whole populations, international travel is possible for many – not just the few – and powerful technology fills the homes of ordinary people. Our lives have been revolutionized by the outputs of scientific research. Now scientists are playing a crucial role concerning the future of the planet, by warning about the consequences – this time for the global climate – of this growth and access to technology. Scientists have been able to suggest the means of ameliorating climate change, and need to be credited with persuading politicians across the world that global warming can be put down to human activity. Truly we really do need science.

However, despite its effectiveness in uncovering the secrets of the physical world, there are many aspects of the social world for which the scientific perspective is less well suited. To the extent that phenomena are technical and rational, scientific practices provide an effective methodology. However, where we wish to engage with the social, emotional or political, science proves more limited. Alvesson and Deetz (2000, p. 49) have argued there has been a growing dissatisfaction among social researchers with what they term 'conventional' approaches to research, dominated as they are by positivistic methods that emphasize objectivity, neutrality, scientific procedure, quantification and hypothesis testing – in other words the scientific approach. There has been a growth in qualitative methodologies, but their 'respectability' remains patchy. Both Alvesson and Deetz (2000) and, in an introduction to a special issue of the journal *Culture and Organization* on the Art of Management and Organisation, Watkins *et al.* (2006), feel that there is a dividing line between emergent European and American traditions. Watkins and colleagues suggest that:

> It would not be unfair to characterise mainstream American scholarship as a continual search to perfect the science-based tools of management and organisation to enable the pursuit of efficiency, performance and this increased profit … In contrast European scholarship is increasingly coming to challenge not only the efficacy but also the suitability of the tools of science, for what they see as an exploration of the complexities of social processes.
>
> (Watkins *et al.*, 2006, p. 1)

However, the situation is paradoxical. The contributions of North American scholars to contemporary developments in qualitative research have been, and continue to be, highly significant. For example, a survey of the roles and places of work of the authors of 44 chapters in the third edition of the authoritative *Sage Handbook of Qualitative Research* (Denzin and Lincoln, 2005) shows that three-quarters are from the United States, with the remainder being divided between European and Australia and the Pacific countries. Several chapters included in Denzin and Lincoln's (2005) book are concerned with what we may see as creative strategies and methods of inquiry, e.g. Alexander (2005) and Finley (2005).

Leaving to one side international differences, the legitimacy of qualitative methodologies may also be questioned within our systems – in the organizations in which we may want to conduct our study; in a range of professional fields;

and in academia. People can hold strong views about what constitutes 'proper' research. Managers in organizations, who have the power to let researchers into, or to exclude them from, their company, may have been academically or professionally educated within a positivist tradition of inquiry. Schön (1987) has argued that much of the education and training of professionals is characterized by technical rationality. Similarly, Roberts (1996) suggested that a great deal of management education and training is rooted in instrumental rationality. Such approaches contain the assumption that there is a fixed body of professional knowledge and techniques that merely have to be learned and then applied. This is true for some academic traditions and professions. This is illustrated both by Graham's story and the reflections of Dr Cecil Helman in the two cases that follow.

A Master's dissertation student's story – Graham

I've just got my MSc now. Phew! But, as it turns out, I was late submitting the dissertation. The other evening I was in the pub with all the other students celebrating their successes, but at that stage, I'd only just started! Why? Because I work in the National Health Service and it took ages to get 'ethical approval' from the health trust. Everyone in the pub was great, and I got congratulated as much as everyone else – just for getting the go-ahead to do the research! Anyway, there's a happy ending to this, but it's interesting to reflect on what happened. I mean I wasn't out to use any outlandish research methods, but I wanted to do the study through qualitative methods. That's what the problem was really. The research governance systems for ethical approval in the health services were set up, quite rightly, to prevent the exploitation of patients and their families in clinical trials. So what we've got is a view that all research should be 'evidence-based' – using control groups, double-blind testing and the like. What I wanted to do was nothing to do with patients, but I wanted to look into nurses' attitudes and feelings about new ways of working, and I wanted to use an action-research framework to do this. Clearly, I work in a system that's used to working in a strong scientific clinical tradition, and qualitative research just simply wasn't well understood or supported. They told me my proposal was too 'touchy-feely' and not valid as research. In the end I was given the go-ahead with only minimal compromise.

Graham did not employ any of the creative methods that we explore in this book, although he was clearly working with a qualitative methodology. His case illustrates that the opportunity to undertake qualitative research is not just predicated on intellectual argument, but potentially also on the belief system of those who hold power in the organization in which the research is to be situated. Graham suffered a painful process of getting approval. However, there was a silver lining to the cloud that hung over the protracted contracting-phase of his research: his critical reflections on his experiences contributed to a wonderful methodology chapter in his dissertation!

'Techno-medicine' v. the personal and the subjective in medicine (Helman, 2006)

The epistemological debates concerning different views of knowledge are not of course confined to organizational research. Dr Helman has spent 27 years as a general practitioner in the London suburbs, and has written widely on his experiences, based on his medical anthropological insights. In his recent book, he reflects on the respective roles that the scientific and the subjective play in the treatment of illness:

> Many of this new breed of specialist and techno-doctor have no time for ... general practitioners, with their broad and unfocused areas of knowledge, their archaic listening skills, their collection of medical tales and quaint medical aphorisms. ... family medicine still holds the personal, the subjective and the social to be important – especially the patients' own narratives of their illnesses, as well as their family 'history'. Sight and hearing and touch are still just as crucial as diagnostic machines. ... Techno-medicine, by contrast, offers us a dream of a world without ambiguity, of a scientific paradise in which everything makes sense, one where almost everything can be measured. ... It's a utopia where Science replaces spirituality, and uncertainty has no place, where the patient's emotions, fears and belief system and spirituality are less important than the printout from a diagnostic machine.... But it's a fantasy, an intellectual cul-de-sac. For in real life the body is not everything and – as I have learned again and again over the years – both ambiguity and uncertainty will always be part of any form of medical practice.
>
> (Helman, 2006, p. 157)

The powerful status of positivism does not just reside in the organizations to be researched. It also features within what has been called the 'patriarchal nature of academic life and the "research infrastructure"' (Punch, 1998, p. 161). Punch suggests that the growth of gender and race research is in part a reaction to the stifling nature of patriarchy in research institutions. Such research is liberationist in aim, to raise consciousness about the many forms of oppression that can exist in organizational settings, including sexism, racism and homophobia. In addition, he observes that this development has had the effect of opening up the available repertoire of approaches to research in social systems and with people, given its explicit concern with affective elements of research, reflexivity and an action orientation. Further, this 'enrichment' has mostly been embedded within qualitative research.

Ann Rippin's experience (Rippin, 2006) is relevant to this discussion in a number of ways. She employs an unconventional arts-based medium in order to research organizations and emotions in organizations, and she provides a vivid example of an academic researcher struggling to locate her work within an academic environment. Ann is an 'academic quilter' She has used the process of making quilts as a way of developing her reflective practice as an academic researcher; as an outlet for creative energy; and as a representation of organization. She argues that to research emotion in some parts of academia can be hard, because emotions can be treated as a taboo, a value-laden concept that implies weakness and disruption of organizational life. Thus:

> The desire to disassociate oneself as an academic from what is weak, illogical, biased and indeed disruptive, is very strong and thus an element of self-policing around what is legitimate in terms of content and methodology becomes almost inevitable.
>
> (Rippin, 2006, p. 34)

She argues that a main reason for this potential self-limiting attitude towards less-conventional research is a powerfully imposed performance culture or mental landscape that is linked to quantifiable performance in which 'there are preferred ways of doing scholarship and research in order to gain advancement ...' (Rippin, 2006, p. 35). Having said this, we can be optimistic about creative approaches. It is clear that Ann has made a contribution to the 'enrichment' that Punch (1998) refers to, as well as to the growth in legitimacy of, and discussion about, creative approaches to research within academia – some of which we reviewed in the introduction (e.g. Fineman, 2000; Finley, 2003; Mullen, 2003; Watkins et al., 2006). Ann tells the story about how she took a deep breath to talk about something very personal to her at the 2002 Art of Management Conference in London, and about how the people who attended her session were:

> more supportive and encouraging than I could ever have imagined, and it is in no small part due to them that I have continued with my practice of making quilts and that I have continued to theorise that practice.
>
> (Rippin, 2006, p. 25)

Academic institutions and research centres consist of staff and powerful actors (tutors, examiners, research committee members) who will hold a range of views about what constitutes good research. In many institutions, there is a creative tension between colleagues as they represent their paradigmic views. Such a climate can hold the prospect of respectful debate and learning, with the recognition that there is a need to listen to, and work with, different perspectives. However, in some other places, the opposite is true – there can be intolerance of the unorthodox and of the experimental, and to begin to think about suggesting dialogue, drama or drawings as the base of one's research will feel risky.

The researcher will realize from the foregoing that the decision to use a creative approach is not a soft option. But the purpose of this discussion is not to discourage. On the contrary, there is a range of arguments that may be put forward in support of the use of creative methods in organizational research. As we have already noted, there is a growing recognition that researching in less orthodox ways is necessary and valid, in part because people's experiences in organizations are becoming more complex. In addition, there is more comprehension – both in the literature and among sponsors of research – about the importance of devising and using different methods for understanding that complexity as people experience it. This often means giving people – research participants – a voice, to be able to express something that they do not often have the opportunity to say, or that is difficult to put into words. Working in these ways gives us at least partial glimpses into truths that would otherwise be unknowable.

We believe that the risks of using creative methods are less now than they used to be, and the rewards – in terms of insight, understanding and potential contribution to knowledge – are greater. It would be unwise to see any research study as one that is going to be simple and straightforward. It would be equally dangerous to enter into these approaches uncritically. But, in their different ways, Sue's and Graham's stories showed that, even if the research experience is characterized by struggle, the potential for learning is high. As a society we need to continue the quest to understand how we are, or are not, in increasingly complex settings and interactions. The creative approaches that we have included here make a contribution to our repertoire of methods – a contribution that enables us and others to comprehend in some depth what is happening.

With the above background in mind, we will discuss the four assumptions that we believe underpin the use of creative methods:

1. An appreciation of the rich and multifaceted dimensions of human experience can make an important contribution to our understanding of social systems.
2. The creative arts can enhance our capacity to find different expressive forms to inquire into human experience.
3. The data that are generated by creative methods often take on metaphorical forms, and metaphor offers insights into organizational experience.
4. Collaborative approaches to inquiry are appropriate for the exploration of human experience.

The ensuing discussion begins the process of laying a philosophical basis for the use of creative methods by arguing that our understanding of social systems can be enhanced by placing human experience at the centre of our work as organizational researchers, and that creative methods have the capacity to enable the expression of voice – about participants' feelings, experiences and recollections – in ways that might otherwise be difficult or unwise.

Research participants can find it productive to express feelings and perceptions through the use of metaphorical devices, e.g. in drawings and poetry, because, we argue, metaphor can act as a container for emotional and unconscious forces at work. We then propose that the use of creative approaches in organizational research is predicated on developing a collaborative relationship with organizations and research participants. In Chapter 2 we will develop our arguments by suggesting the forms of critical awareness that the organizational researcher needs to develop if she or he is to use creative methods effectively and ethically.

MULTIFACETED DIMENSIONS OF HUMAN EXPERIENCE

We start with the assumption that the research of social systems can be enhanced by giving attention to the rich and multifaceted dimensions of human experience. This experience can take the form of a fleeting or momentary event (such as Munch's sudden onset of anxiety), or may be characterized by deep and long-held aspect of our lives, like our relationships with others, or our sense of role and identity. Human beings have complex emotional lives, do not always behave rationally, and are not always easily understood. Orthodox thinking about organization has been based on rational and analytical models in which the place for feelings and emotions in organizational life has been denied or marginalized. Taylorism, Fordism and other forms of bureaucratic and mechanistic organization, with their emphasis on conformity, systems, depersonalized production and processes of control, have dominated our thinking and understanding. The reader will notice that we return regularly to the notion that creative methods enable management and organizational researchers in a collaborative inquiring relationship with research participants, to access a richer, fuller life which includes understanding more about basic human yearnings (Windle, 2006 – see Chapter 6) and a life and dimension beyond that reached by the written word alone (Etherington, 2004 – see Chapter 8). In Chapter 8, as part of our review, we will build on Reason's (2001) suggestion that creative methods enable researchers and participants to access a richer, deeper, more true-to-life and more useful 'knowing' if this is constituted in a complex relationship between different forms of knowing.

Antonacopoulou and Bento (2004) work in the field of leadership development, and have noted the recent increased interest in exploring the relationships between arts and management. They especially pointed to the efforts of leadership developers to engage with poetry, painting and music as ways of illuminating management and leadership (p. 93). And, adopting Marcic's (2002) arguments, they suggest that traditional management paradigms underutilize the:

> multiple intelligences of organization members by only addressing the rational approaches to leadership development and leaving aside the aesthetic and emotional dimensions that are so critical to self awareness
>
> (Marcic, 2002, p. 93)

Crotty (1998, p. 83) sees research that is geared towards collecting and analysing data of a subjective nature as being central to a phenomenological/interpretivist methodology, that is the study of people's subjective and everyday experience. He suggests that a major feature of this approach is the attempt by the researcher to see it from the participant's point of view and to minimize the imposition of the researcher's suppositions. Researchers working from these assumptions will be wary about imposing meanings or constructions on the emergent data, and instead will wish to 'intuit' the data and invite others, including the research participants themselves, to join the process of pointing to the themes that are genuinely contained in the data. Thus, Crotty suggests, subjectivist research of this kind emerges as an exploration, via personal experience, of prevailing cultural understandings.

We are therefore interested in researching (with participants) into a range of facets of lived experience, including recollections, stories about significant events, and emotions. In his seminal edited text, Fineman (1993) argued that:

> Writers on organizations have successfully 'written out' emotions ... We teach and preach on organizational life and management, usually acknowledging that our subject matter can be a bit messy – because people are not like machines. But at the same time we fail to square up to the essential emotionality of organizational processes, much of which is, and is likely to remain, unmanaged.
>
> (Fineman, 1993, p. 1)

In the introduction to his subsequent edition, Fineman (2000) noted that the study of emotion in organizations has become an 'expanding arena' (Fineman, 2000, p. 1), a sub-discipline in the study of organizations. But he also reviewed the development since the early 1990s of a range of other associated trends that add to our capacity to understand more about organizational experience (Fineman, 1993, pp. 1–3):

- Increased concern with emotionalized issues, such as workplace envy, intimacy, harassment, stress
- The popularization of 'emotional intelligence'

- A concern with aesthetics and emotion, the meaning that we sometimes invest in material objects at work
- Growth of a social constructionist approach
- Continuing prevalence of psychoanalytical approaches – the role that repressed thoughts, unconscious defences and fantasies play among people and groups in organizational life.

It is important to say that Fineman examined these trends more critically and thoroughly than we are able to do here. Our intention, however, is to point to the idea that multidimensional and multifaceted experiences of organizational life are reflected by a diverse set of theoretical 'takes' on the nature of lived experience in social settings. Of course there is a legitimate and sometimes necessary set of rational/positivist lenses through which the researcher can understand and evaluate experience, for example when cool detached inquiry or evaluation is required. But a concern with researching the lived experiences of organizational members and managers leads us more often than not to expressions of their sometimes unstated 'gut feels', anxieties and stories.

The creative methods that we discuss are intended to enable people to find their expressive capacities concerning subjective and emotional data that are not always easy to access. Our argument is that data that take the form of expression or portraying of the subjective and personal are valid. The adoption of creative approaches to inquiry within an interpretivist and collaborative approach contributes to our ability to learn more about the subjective experience of individuals – their feelings, recollections, reflections and attitudes, for example. Our aim is to understand the ways in which organizational members and groups of individuals create, interpret, and give meaning to, the world in which they work and live.

FINDING DIFFERENT EXPRESSIVE FORMS

Effective use of creative methods can put the organizational researcher in a position to enable participants to find and use their voices – to be able to express their feelings, recollections and reflections of organizational experience when it may be difficult to do so in other circumstances. This is not because we regard participants' voices as mere empirical data. Participants' voices are of course 'data', but, we suggest, it goes deeper than this, because of our wish to work respectfully with the issues and feelings that people have in organizations, just as we have such issues and feelings ourselves. This is influenced in part by a value that participants may have something important to say and that they should have a chance to say it. Sometimes the structures and implicit rules of organizations do not always allow them to verbalize experience and feelings, or only to express them with a controlled and inauthentic voice. Marcic (2002), for example, has described the tendency of organizational leaders and managers to rely on self-presentation routines that are based in their competence and expertise.

Creative research may offer a way to speak and to be heard from a more vulnerable and emotional place.

The concern with participant voice is not one that is confined to creative approaches, and it is characteristic of a range of qualitative research traditions. We will consider two of these here – feminist research and participatory action research. Thus, Olesen (1998) argued, for example, that the question of voice, and the nature of the accounts that research participants can or do give about their experiences, are a major focus of concern to feminist researchers. She argues that, for some feminist researchers the main methodological question concerns 'how voices of participants are to be heard, with what authority, and in what form' (1998, p. 318). This question, she continues, stems from a critical analysis of orthodox qualitative research, where a relative absence, or distortion, of women's voices can be noted, and:

> the charge that … the account in the usual social science modes only replicates hierarchical conditions found in the parent discipline, where women are outside the account.
>
> (Olesen, 1998, p. 318)

Olesen continued by arguing that there is a need to develop innovative ways and new textual and presentational practices (such as poetry, dramatic readings, and the telling of personal stories) to reflect and present voice.

Enabling the expression of voice is also a basis of participatory action research which takes on an emancipatory or liberationist view of the purpose of inquiry. Just one example of this is provided by Douglas (2002), who recounted the setting up of a black women managers' co-operative inquiry group that was intended to explore strategies for 'moving from surviving to thriving'. The main aim of the project was to create more understanding about how change-agents might more effectively impact on institutional discrimination. Her aim was to shift the traditional power balance by using her research as a vehicle for the voices and thoughts of black women to be expressed. This stemmed from a belief that 'years of witnessing, observing and experiencing discrimination' had developed in black women (in this instance) a 'sixth sense' that allowed them to 'know' discrimination, even when they were not able to verbalize the problem objectively.

The study of organizations – and finding and enabling different expressive forms with participants – can, we believe, be enriched by seeing what other branches of human endeavour, including the arts, have to offer the researcher. In his earlier work, Fineman suggested that, as researchers, we:

> can be more adventurous in our use of available media such as photographs, drawings and paintings – less conventional vehicles in a word-occupied publication culture. … mediums of art and humanities are used to address the expressive limitations of the conventional written text. … Inventing

> new expressive forms, or adopting ones from other disciplines, is liberating
> for the student of emotions.
>
> (Fineman, 1993, p. 222)

We noted in the introduction that Fineman (2000, p. 15) suggested that we can learn from the poet, novelist and dramatist, so that we can find 'different voices, or expressive forms, to convey crucial experiences and meanings'. Bochner and Ellis (2003) argued similarly that we might 'blur the boundaries' between social sciences and humanities by using novel forms of expressing lived experience, with advantage:

> We have used and encouraged other researchers to use novel forms for
> expressing lived experience including literary, fictional, poetic, autoethno-
> graphic, visual, performative, and co-constructed modes of narration.
>
> (Bochner and Ellis, 2003, p. 509)

Bochner's and Ellis' goal in their research has been to produce stories that show the width and depth of the complexities of lived experience, including:

> moments of struggle, resisting the intrusions of chaos, disconnection,
> fragmentation, marginalization, and incoherence, trying to preserve or
> restore the continuity and coherence of life's unity in the face of
> unexpected blows of fate that call one's meanings and values into question.
>
> (Bochner and Ellis, 2003, p. 509)

They noted that although they had both been trained as scientists, their work had brought them closer and closer to the worlds of art, poetry, and literature. They also felt that the results of narratives based in art, poetry, and literature, could be judged by how well they enable us to understand, feel, and grapple with the experiences being expressed. Similarly, Finley (2005) supports arguments that hold:

> that there are varied ways in which the world can be known and that
> broadening the range of perspectives available for constructing knowledge
> increases the informative value of research.
>
> (Finley, 2005, p. 685)

Thus, she continues, researchers are increasingly using art forms that include visual and performing arts as well as forms borrowed from literature. There is a sense therefore of boundary-crossing between different branches of human and social endeavour that entails, according to Finley, a critique of language-based ways of knowing.

METAPHOR IN ORGANIZATIONAL AND MANAGEMENT RESEARCH

When Shakespeare wrote 'All the world's a stage ...' he was using metaphor. A characteristic of the data that are generated through the use of the creative methods is that they often take on metaphorical forms. Thus, when research participants produce drawings that tell us something about their lived experience, they may very well produce visual metaphors (Chapter 4). Metaphor pervades poetic forms of expression (Chapter 6), and the notion of the organization as theatre or drama lies at the heart of the discussion in Chapter 7. When we talk about something (an experience or a person for example) as if it were another thing, we attempt to describe meaning or gain understanding. Much of the time, we *think* in metaphor. For example, a group of managers talking about a recent experience which entailed a high degree of anxiety began to make frequent references to being on an 'emotional roller-coaster' and on a 'white-knuckle ride' – metaphors that are used quite frequently by people in turbulent and changing organizations. Such metaphors can suggest different levels of meaning that may be held unconsciously by participants. In this example, we might inquire into the 'super-metaphor' of the adventure park, and ask whether this is somehow representative of the organization's culture ('adventure': in the sense of what comes, or happens, to us, by chance; or to be adventurous, innovative or experimental). Similarly, when a person is described as being 'a terrier at the meeting', this is a metaphorical expression to show tenacity.

All language is based on metaphor – even if the underlying metaphors have often faded and become lost. For many people, the encounter with metaphor in the study of literature has obscured just how pervasive metaphors are. The use of metaphor always implies a way of seeing and thinking – in other words, it is the way in which, in everyday life, we put our theories into words; that is, even when we do not think that we are theorizing. All theory is metaphor; all metaphor is theory. We live and think by metaphor (Lakoff and Johnson, 1980; Grant and Oswick, 1996). Morgan (2006) suggests that metaphors provide ways of seeing and thinking about organizations:

> all theories of organisation and management are based on implicit images or metaphors that lead us to see, understand and manage organizations in distinctive yet partial ways.
>
> (Morgan, 2006, p. 4)

Burke (1992) went as far as to say that metaphors are windows into the soul of the social system. However, while metaphor has the capacity to cause us to look and think differently, it can also obscure. We can use the metaphor of theatre to illustrate this (Chapter 7). As the curtains and lights go up on the scene being researched, the stage and actors are in the spotlight, but the wider surroundings within which the

performance is witnessed is in darkness. Thus, wider systemic and cultural influences may be hidden from view. It is interesting to see that metaphor itself can become a mask that reveals and conceals.

Metaphor provides a description of something by reference to another object that is different from, but analogous to, the 'something' originally described. This is particularly valuable when researching organizational experience, because metaphors can act as a container for emotional and unconscious forces at work. Such data can often be heard more easily than rational explanations, and they invite interaction among research participants, or between the researcher and a participant, because the symbolism seems creative – playful even. They provide vivid, memorable and emotion-arousing representations of preconceived experience. Averill (1990) suggests that emotional aspects of experience that are difficult to contain, often become the subjects of metaphor. In organizations, where direct expressions of emotion can be suppressed and avoided, individual and organizational defences against emotion become very powerful. It is rather like looking directly into the eyes of Medusa: the fear of emotion can turn organizational members to stone. Metaphors may therefore serve a reflecting function, allowing the participant to look indirectly at powerful emotions without being turned to stone; and they can provide an opportunity for research participants to look indirectly at unconscious forces at work (Broussine and Vince, 1995).

Case study: Cinderella (Celia's story)

Sometimes metaphor calls to us in a manner which is hard to ignore. Such was the case in the analysis of an interview I undertook with a social worker as part of a study into the identities of social workers (Keeping, 2006). Having described the many difficulties within her multidisciplinary team, her concluding sentence was:

> It would be nice if we could get a bit more respect. You feel like you're in a Cinderella profession don't you?

This led me to consider the fairy-tale as a metaphor for the account given by the interviewee. What started as a playful musing, to my surprise, ended up illuminating in a particularly creative and, at times humorous way, key elements of the experiences of this social worker and of many others in the study. The respondent told a sorry story. In her place of work she was greatly outnumbered by health professionals, and she experienced a great deal of difficulty in getting her voice heard. She felt strongly that she was not offered the respect that was due to her and other social workers, and as a group they were not valued by their

health colleagues. As she put it:

> In terms of how you're respected and your status, you are at the bottom
> of the pile, which is not great.

Although she was proud of being a social worker, she was very aware of the lack of respect afforded the profession by the general public, the media and other members of the team. This lack of respect appeared to be connected to a lack of personal self-worth and an underplaying of the high level of skill required to carry out the complexities of the social work task, e.g. sensitivity, use of authority, knowledge of the law, capacity to deal with powerful emotions, difficult dilemmas, and sheer hard work. Yet she undermined herself and the task, deriding her motivations for embarking on a career in social work:

> I've always been that kind of person, rescuing small animals and stuff
> like that [laugh] ... sounds really sad [laugh]. It sounds like the Miss
> World competition – I like helping people across the road [laugh], but
> I just really like helping people and feeling like I've made a difference.

I was struck by the use of traditional feminine roles, and also noted the physical appearance of this respondent – that of a young, softly spoken attractive woman with long blonde hair, and these factors undoubtedly fuelled my associations with the Cinderella story. Playing around with the story and its possible application to the experience of this social worker was surprisingly useful in encapsulating her experience. As we know, Cinderella was relegated to the kitchen and menial work, being afforded none of the privileges and status of her rank. This social worker felt relegated also to the 'menial' tasks of administration, her views being disregarded, even about those service users whom she knew well. The community psychiatric nurses and consultant psychiatrist – the ugly sisters and step-mother? – were experienced as powerful agents within the team, who colluded in undermining and bullying the respondent. The situation was reinforced by the public image of social workers – who, after all, respects a kitchen maid? Cinderella's kindly yet ineffectual and emasculated father did nothing to protect his daughter, just as the 'parental' employers of social workers do little to protect and promote the voice of social work. This father-figure could also represent the weak and undeveloped masculine aspect of Cinderella's personality, and could be useful in understanding the state of mind of this very feminine and self-deprecating respondent.

Despite her tendency to undermine herself within a profession suffering from a significant image problem, this social worker expressed strong views about the

Continued

worth of social work. She felt that, just as social workers were devalued and their opinions disregarded, so the needs and wishes of her service users were ignored and undermined. Just as Cinderella held on to her dream, so this social worker held on to something precious which saw her through the darkest days of work. She felt that the therapeutic relationship with the service user was at the heart of social work, and the one aspect which gave her job (and indeed her life, given her identification with service users and her deeply held beliefs) meaning. Without this, she felt that her job was without hope. Thus, we have the dream of true love and the dream of therapeutic connection serving to rescue both Cinderella and our social worker respectively from oppressive and seemingly hopeless situations.

The story provides further metaphor material. Who does the fairy godmother represent? The pumpkin-turned-carriage? The ecstatic dancing with the Prince? The lost slipper? Playing with these metaphors provided a new perspective on my interview data, and drawing on a story such as Cinderella, epitomizing, as it does, the triumph of right over wrong, provided hope and an opening up of possibilities. The creative space opened up by using metaphor has the potential for developing our material in unforeseen ways and freeing us to play around with meanings and associations in a way that can enrich and develop our work. It can also be fun!

COLLABORATIVE FORMS OF INQUIRY FOR THE EXPLORATION OF HUMAN EXPERIENCE

So far, we have explored how people's realities are subjective and multiple, and how the researcher needs to interact with the research participant in order to gain some access to these realities. Our fourth assumption is that collaborative forms of inquiry are appropriate for the exploration of human experience. Dr Helman earlier provided us with a useful analogy to help us make our argument. He maintained that sight, hearing and touch have a crucial part to play in the general practitioner's relationship with his or her patients, and indeed that the GP can gain a holistic view of the patient's experience by taking in the emotional and subjective information that may emerge in the doctor–patient relationship. Similarly, a basis of our argument is that organizational researchers will gain a deeper and broader understanding of what is happening to research participants by getting alongside them (i.e. in a collaborative and participative relationship), rather than researching them from afar through methodologies that 'subject' them to scrutiny – whatever the paradigm adopted. So, the belief held by researchers committed to collaborative forms of inquiry (e.g. Marshall and Reason, 1998; Reason, 1998a; Heron and Reason, 2001) is that, instead of depending on questionnaires and similar instrumentation-based methodologies, we should rely on the self-directing person as the primary

source of knowing and thus the main 'instrument' of inquiry. As Peter Reason has stated:

> on the one hand the scientific perspective has taught us the value of critical public testing of what is taken as knowledge, another consequence has been to place the researcher firmly outside and separate from the subject of his or her research, reaching for an objective knowledge and for one separate truth. I believe and hope that there is an emerging worldview, more holistic, pluralist and egalitarian that is essentially participative.
>
> (Reason, 1998b, pp. 261–262)

The implication of such arguments was put succinctly by Heron and Reason (2001, p. 179), as follows:

> We believe that good research is research conducted *with* people rather than *on* people [their emphases]

Peter Reason (1998a, p. 149) tells the story about how he 'got into' *co-operative* inquiry (his preferred term):

> I think at first I saw co-operative inquiry as simply a way to get data which was both more 'accurate' because it was based directly on experience, and also more ethical since it engaged with people rather than did research on people. At this level participation is merely a methodological issue. Then, influenced by my reading of PAR [participative action research] and feminist literature, and my involvement in peer learning communities, I realized that participation also involved peoples' right and ability to have a say in decisions which affect them, and thus as well as being a methodological nicety is a *political imperative* [his emphasis].

This political imperative originates in humanistic psychology (Reason, 1998b, p. 264), a belief that people are entitled to decide how they live their own lives, free from conditioning and restrictive social customs; and working together with others should entail norms of openness. Such beliefs led to a critique of orthodox forms of research, especially the assertion that conventional social science had excluded human beings from the thinking about how the research is to be conducted and about how conclusions were to be drawn from the data. From this critique emerged the notion of co-operative inquiry, sometimes known as collaborative inquiry (CI), a fundamental tenet of which is the idea that people should be invited to participate in the co-creation of knowing about themselves, rather than have interpretations and meanings about their experience imposed by the researchers.

Marshall and Reason (1998) argued that collaborative forms of inquiry put us in a position where, among other things, we can work with emergent research methodologies, that is that this type of relationship with and between research participants seems to facilitate experimentation with different research methodologies. In this context, they mention story-telling, psycho-drama, circle dancing, and various exercises and approaches to working with qualitative data. In part, this was because their students were able to contribute and develop ideas about such methodologies with each other. Thus, the framework enabled both explanation and expression as alternative modes of working with qualitative data in sense-making, but the value of expression was particularly affirmed.

CONCLUSION

We are not arguing that only a CI approach is the sole condition for the effective use of creative methods. We acknowledge the significant influences of CI advocates on our own practice, values and ways of seeing organizational research. Of course, co-operative inquiry groups are, as we have learned from Marshall and Reason (1998), arenas that potentially encourage the use of creative methods. However, we do not envisage that the use of creative methods can be confined to particular forms of inquiry like CI. Our preference is therefore to talk about a *collaborative approach*, which we see as a principled and reflexive relationship between researcher and research participants that gives the best conditions for using creative methods. Securing, agreeing and working with these conditions is nearly always problematic, and requires a *collaborative awareness* that is in part pragmatic, and requires some leadership on the part of the researcher, as well as a political sensitivity to what may be possible or otherwise in certain sites of inquiry. In large measure this is an issue of power – the power to define what is knowledge and whose reality is the right or best reality. Researching with people requires us to maintain a reflexive capacity; to always hold in view the relationship between power and knowledge; and to find our role and sense of validity in the process without denying the role and validity of others. Working with these dilemmas and challenges requires that we develop a capacity for critical subjectivity and awareness. We will be saying more about this topic in Chapter 2.

As well as the important theoretical and ethical considerations that we have considered in this chapter, there is also a strong pragmatic argument for adopting collaborative approaches with participants that we want to emphasize, that such approaches tend to be useful because they also speed up the process of establishing researcher–participant rapport and trust, and that therefore they are faster at generating richer empirical material about human experience. The management or organizational researcher needs to be principled as she or he conducts the study, but this does not mean that accessing data about lived experience needs to be inefficient.

DISCUSSION QUESTIONS

1. What forms of possible resistance to the use of creative research methods might the organizational and management researcher meet when seeking access to undertake a study?
2. Why might the use of creative methods sit uneasily within a positivist/scientific research paradigm?
3. What is the case against using creative methods in organization and management research?
4. Why is a collaborative relationship between the researcher and the research participant one that is likely to be fruitful for experimentation with different methods of inquiry?

FURTHER READING

Matts Alvesson's and Stan Deetz's (2000) book provides the opportunity to understand more about what is distinctive about management research, and about the fundamentals of critical research. The authors warn that theirs is not a text for the novice, and it assumes, like our book, that the reader has some prior knowledge about qualitative research. However, we recommend it here because, as will become clear as the reader proceeds through our book (see Chapter 2), we regard the development of critical awareness on the part of the researcher as central to an effective use of creative management and organizational research methods. Alvesson and Deetz provide a critical overview of 'quantitative and conventional qualitative methodology', and, for illustration, in Chapter 3 of their book they focus on the 'sorry state of the art of leadership research' as well as other topics relevant to management, such as motivation and organization structures. It is therefore a provocative book, and part of the provocation lies in the argument that too much research tries to simplify explanations of phenomena rather than provide multiple ways of understanding.

Gareth Morgan's classic book on metaphors, originally published in 1986, has been updated in a 2006 edition, and, given the importance that we place on metaphor as one of our key underpinnings for creative research methods, we recommend that the reader visits his book to become (re)acquainted with this way of seeing and thinking about organizations. The imagery that he employs as he sets out the various metaphorical takes of organization provided an early source of inspiration for many of the contributors to the present book.

There are many sources that the researcher can consult about research paradigms and ways of knowing, and a small range of these are mentioned in this book. However, Dr Cecil Helman's book, as well as providing some poignant and funny stories about his experience as a general practitioner in London – and this aspect alone

provides reason enough to get hold of this delightful book – gives us an insight into the contested paradigms employed in medicine. His distinction between 'techno-medicine' and holistic medicine provides a wonderful insight into epistemological debate and the feelings that this provokes.

Alvesson, M. and Deetz, S. (2000) *Doing Critical Management Research*, London: Sage Publications

Helman, C. (2006) *Suburban Shaman: Tales from Medicine's Front Line*, London: Hammersmith Press

Morgan, G. (2006) *Images of Organization*, Thousand Oaks, CA: Sage Publications

THE SEDUCTIVE QUALITIES OF CREATIVE METHODS: CRITICAL AWARENESS

Mike Broussine

OVERVIEW

- **Researching respectfully, ethically and responsibly**
- **Methodological awareness**
- **Critical self-awareness and reflexivity**
- **Collaborative awareness**
- **Ethical awareness**
- **Critical data awareness and validity**
- **Conclusion**
- **Discussion questions**
- **Further reading**

This chapter is about researching respectfully, ethically and responsibly. The use of creative methods suggests a set of researcher responsibilities, capacities and sets of critical awareness about methodology, self in the research process, the researcher/participant relationship, ethics, and about the nature of the data that may be generated. These five forms of awareness together enable the researcher to build a capacity for critical consciousness about what she or he is doing through all stages of the research. We discuss the types of researcher capacity that we feel are necessary in the management of creative and collaborative research relationships, and examine the notion of researcher reflexivity. This capacity, and the associated forms of awareness, will apply to any form of research, whether or not creative methods are used. But, just as other means of getting data require their own particular sets of responsibilities, disciplines, and rigour – consider the processes involved in gathering

and validating statistical data, for example – so creative approaches make their own special demands on the researcher. Creative methods have the potential to uncover some powerful emotions, stories and dramas, and therefore this chapter discusses how we may work with participants responsibly. Thus, we continue the process begun in Chapter 1 by dealing with some further principles about the use of creative methods in organizational research. Further, we continue to share our own learning journey about these topics, processes and capacities. In the chapters that follow, we will be pointing out specific implications that apply to a particular creative method.

METHODOLOGICAL AWARENESS

Decisions about methodology are fundamental. Ontological and epistemological assumptions play a key role in arriving at these decisions. Easterby-Smith *et al.* (2004, p. 27) suggest that there are three reasons why an understanding of research philosophical issues is important:

- because such an understanding can clarify research designs;
- it helps the researcher to recognize which designs work or do not work;
- it may help the researcher to identify or create designs that may be outside his or her past experiences.

We suggest that critically aware organizational or management researchers try to work consciously with the 'baggage' and biases that shape our assumptions. In these ways they can put themselves into a position where they can defend their methodological decisions. We suggested in Chapter 1 that creative methods sit uneasily within a positivist paradigm, and much of the researcher's methodological awareness will most likely flow from an elemental inclination to work within an interpretivist methodology (Crotty, 1998). Alvesson and Deetz (2000, pp. 33–34) add some useful additional pointers about the nature of interpretivist research. For such researchers:

- The organization is a social site – the emphasis is on the social rather than the economic
- People are not considered to be objects, but rather active sense-makers along with the researcher
- Key conceptions and understandings (theory) are worked out with the research participants who can 'collaborate in displaying key features of their world' (Alvesson and Deetz, 2000, p. 34)
- The aim is to see how people's realities are socially produced
- The purpose of research is to capture a complex and creative 'life form' 'that may be lost to modern, instrumental life or overlooked by it' (Alvesson and Deetz, 2000, p. 34).

Methodological awareness enables us to account for ourselves as researchers, and this is the purpose of methodology chapters in dissertations, theses and research reports. We need to be able to 'show our hand', and give as transparent an explanation as possible about our methodological decisions and assumptions. This applies to all research, but what we need to examine are the special implications of choosing a creative approach.

Mike's story

See it from the research supervisor's point of view. A student comes to see you one day with an idea for her dissertation. She has a gleam in her eye, and is clearly full of enthusiasm: 'Yes', she says. 'I know what I'm going to do now – I want to use poetry and stories'. 'Great', you say, 'Why?' 'I like poetry and stories! Besides they seem like fun ways of doing research'. 'OK, let's talk …'.

Confining ourselves for the moment to the research student and supervisor relationship, research supervisors are alert to the possible paradoxes that lie underneath the student's enthusiasm for creative methods in organizational and management research. On one hand, the student's enthusiasm may be based in a well-meaning innocence and inexperience, where anticipation of the 'fun element' masks the care that is required in using these approaches. On the other hand, a student's enthusiasm needs to be welcomed and nourished. Undertaking a research study that in any way requires a sustained level of commitment and energy needs at least some curiosity about the phenomena to be studied, and about the methodologies and methods to be employed. Certainly if the study is going to be a prolonged affair, requiring a long-term commitment over a few months or even years – like undertaking a PhD – some passion about the topic is required.

The main danger of being seduced by the supposed 'fun element', for example, is that the researcher may employ creative methods in an unaware and uncritical way. Such methods have a lot going for them. They may be really engaging for both the researcher and research participant alike. They represent potentially powerful methods for accessing data concerning emotions and other complex manifestations of lived experience. It might appeal that their use is still relatively unusual, particularly given the continuing authority that is ascribed to methods based in positivism. And creative approaches may hold some consonance with one's aesthetic or artistic inclinations.

Thus, the seductive nature of the approaches is both their strength and their weakness. Earlier in this section, the reader may have been struck by the language that we used about undertaking research – describing it as an *affair* that requires *commitment* underpinned by *passion*. Seduction contains the prospect of both something different

and enticing, but also of the danger of being beguiled into an abandonment of principles. This is what the researcher needs to be alert to, and what this chapter will concentrate on. The main message is – by all means be seduced, but do so with a critical eye open!

CRITICAL SELF-AWARENESS AND REFLEXIVITY

The importance of reflexivity in research continues to be discussed and argued about in a number of intellectual streams concerned with social research, including feminist and psychosocial research. The capacity for *reflexivity* lies at the heart of critical self-awareness. Easterby-Smith and Malina (1999) thought that the starting point for understanding reflexivity was the idea that it is not possible for social researchers to be detached from what they are observing. This will be clear from our earlier exploration about the researcher –participant relationship (a matter that we develop in this chapter). To be reflexive requires us to be critical of the assumptions that we may hold, and to be open to learning, possibility and surprise. These kinds of ideas have found expression in feminist and race studies, in which the right of researchers to impose frameworks on less-powerful groups has been challenged (see, for example, Eichler, 1988). Similarly, Easterby-Smith *et al.* (2004, p. 59) have observed that most empirical research in the social sciences has been carried out on members of society who are less powerful than the researchers. The fact that organizational researchers working in the interpretivist paradigm are encouraged to work in a reflexive way with their own experience and their own power when they engage with an organization and the people who belong to it, calls into question our ability to remain value-free and detached.

Etherington suggests that there is a range of ways in which reflexivity can be thought about. She argues (2004, p. 31) that for some researchers, reflexivity is little more than a means of checking for biases in the conduct of research. For others, reflexivity becomes the primary methodological vehicle for inquiry, e.g. in autoethnographic and autobiographical inquiries. Etherington thus demonstrates that we cannot talk simply about reflexivity, but about *reflexivities*. She herself thinks of researcher reflexivity as:

> the capacity of the researcher to acknowledge how their own experiences and contexts (which may be fluid and changing) inform the process and outcomes of inquiry.
>
> (Etherington, 2004, pp. 31–32)

Essentially, the capacity for critical self-awareness and reflexivity in the research process challenges the researcher to be transparent about where she or he is coming from, and to work explicitly and in an 'unsettling' way (Pollner, 1991) with her or

his presuppositions or 'baggage'. We are also attracted to Jessop's (2002) notion of reflexivity as being:

> the ability and commitment to uncover and make explicit to oneself the nature of one's intentions, projects, and actions and their conditions of possibility; and, in this context, to learn about them, critique them, and act upon any lessons that have been learnt
>
> (Jessop, 2002, p. 1)

The research supervision or mentoring process may be a good way to tease out these factors, including critically reflecting on the researcher's previous experiences (e.g. career, life experiences, previous research experiences), ethical stances, political beliefs, and attachments to the proposed topic or site of inquiry. His or her knowledge of, and commitment to, a set of epistemological and methodological assumptions will be important facets of critical self-awareness. The researcher's personal history may contain experiences that she or he brings consciously or unconsciously to the study. We share here a potent experience which contributed significantly to our own learning about researcher awareness. A co-researcher had been deeply and personally affected by earlier experiences of being bullied in an organization. Our research unexpectedly threw up difficult data about bullying in the organizations that took part in our study. The colleague's earlier experiences clearly had the potential to affect our analysis of the data. The fact that he could be explicit with co-researchers about these experiences of being bullied enabled us to work together effectively on the sometimes painful data that we were getting about bullying. What we learned from this episode was that the idea is not to censor out our attachments and earlier experiences, but to put them on the table, and to recognize that it is not always possible for researchers to be unaffected by what they are observing. We are, after all, only human. In general, the purpose of critical self-awareness is to be able to be clear to oneself, to the readers or clients of the eventual publication, thesis or research report, and (most importantly) to your research participants, about what the researcher brings to the research.

As we have said, the organizational and management researcher may have leanings towards creative approaches because of an earlier or current interest in poetry, in art and so on. She or he may have been 'good at ... art/poetry/literature/drama' at school, and may take an ontological position that there is such a thing as an aesthetic value that can form part of our belief system along with other views about the world. This belief system may dispose the researcher towards an attitude about works of art (of whatever kind), and even about how people *should* view art. This may be all well and good, but a self-aware researcher may ask him or herself if she or he is entitled to impose such values, and inquiry processes based on these, on potential research participants. Such leanings or attachments will form part of the material needed to engage in a process of reflexive self-analysis. During our own process of writing this

book – in which we set out our enthusiasm for creative methods – we have had to remind ourselves from time to time about the presuppositions and belief systems that lie at the basis of our arguments. We also have had to take the occasional reflexive turn and remember that, firstly, not everyone shares our enthusiasm, and secondly, that there are other ways of researching the human experience of organizations. Finally, we might consider that we are writing this book, and conducting our research, in a particular culture and social milieu, and that there may be different assumptions about the world and how facets of it may be expressed aesthetically in different cultures.

COLLABORATIVE AWARENESS

We have argued that a collaborative relationship with research participants is a prerequisite for using creative methods. This is not just a methodological issue, important as this is. Just as important is that the nature of the relationship between the researcher and participant is an expression of value – to carry out research *with* people rather than *on* them. As Marshall and Reason (1998, p. 234) put it:

> Collaborative practice demands … an integration of authentic, vulnerable authority with respect for individual autonomy and choice. It is not an easy formula to apply, but requires much skilled attention.

Having established this underlying assumption, we turn now to an exploration of a range of factors that together build a picture of this third aspect of a researcher's critical consciousness. The development of collaborative relations with participants and their organizations requires a sophisticated process that includes attending to:

• The researcher's *leadership* of, and *power* in, the research process; and,
• The *politics* involved in gaining access to organizations and developing a relationship with participants.

Taken together, these two aspects present the researcher with a number of paradoxes which require a developed capacity for critical awareness as we attempt to steer through the questions that arise about our role. For example, as we examine the first of these – the researcher's leadership role and power – we are presented by an interesting question: how can we square the notion of adopting a collaborative approach with the fact that the researcher may have initiated the research? Is it possible to acknowledge one's leadership and power in the process without negating research participants' rights and interpretations? Even when we begin with the intention of researching in a collaborative relationship, the assumption of primacy of our knowledge can emerge. Subtle pressures can grow in the moments of interaction between the researcher and participant or group of participants. Something can happen that leads us, perhaps unconsciously, to diminish the participant's role in the

inquiry. For example, Blumberg and Golembiewski (discussing group experiential learning) talked about the 'real danger' in our encounters with participants that:

> when we bring a person up to a point of discovery, and just as he [sic] is about to make the discovery, we tell him what it is. We deny him the discovery experience
>
> (Blumberg and Golembiewski, 1976, p. 30)

The collaborative nature of the relationship comes into question – we begin to do research 'on' people. This is an issue of power – the power to define what is knowledge and whose reality is the right or best reality. The result is that research becomes 'objective', 'outsider' research that privileges the knowledge and interpretations of the 'expert researcher'.

Therefore the effective management of power and knowledge with participants is central to the development of an effective relationship. We will argue later that our aim in this kind of research is to maintain a dialogic state with participants, so that we do not just see the research output consisting solely of the interpretations and meanings arrived at by the researcher, but to work simultaneously and iteratively with participants' interpretations; the impact of the experience upon them; and what they take away from the experience of participating in the research. Researching with people thus requires us to maintain a reflexive capacity; to always hold in view the relationship between power and knowledge; and to find our role and sense of validity in the process without denying the role and validity of others. As Marshall and Reason (1998) implied, there are no easy answers to such questions, but we suggest that the very fact of asking such questions of oneself, making these paradoxes explicit, for example, in sessions with a research supervisor and with participants themselves, shows a capacity for critical awareness.

Another call on the researcher's potential leadership of a research process is that the research may, to begin with, create anxiety among potential research participants. This anxiety needs to be worked with in the researcher–participant relationship. If this is not attended to, it is possible that the researcher (and participants) 'lose the plot' altogether. Paul's story illustrates the kinds of binds that we can get into if we lose our sense of role and do not effectively manage the relationship with the research group.

Paul's story

On the day of the second research workshop, I was presented with a misunderstanding by the manager about the purpose of the workshop. He introduced

Continued

it as one in which 'Paul will give us feedback on his research so far, and bring us up-to-date on the latest thinking about the management of change' (or some such phrase – his introduction took place before I had got agreement to turn the tape-recorder on). In fact, I thought I had made it clear, both at the time of the first workshop and then in writing, that this second event formed part of the data-gathering phase, and wasn't a review of the whole project as he had thought. When I said that I did not see the workshop in the way he saw it at all, the manager became angry, and even though after a while he grudgingly allowed me to proceed with the workshop as planned, the formerly co-operative relationship I had with participants was contaminated by this misunderstanding and the anxiety it provoked in everyone present. My anxiety about the manager's anger stuck, and I found myself trying to deal with this anxiety as well as the research task. The way I tried to manage this was to offer (too many) views and comments on what was being said, in a hopeless attempt to appease the manager, e.g. stating how this compared with the other participating organizations, references to theory, and the like. This was a doubly unskilled thing to do, since it became clear that participants, including the manager, were beginning to achieve the objectives of this second workshop in their engagement with each other. My losing clarity about my role and purpose on the day, and my confused behaviour as a result of the surprise the manager had presented, led me to think at the time that this workshop was dreadfully ineffective. Having said that, my re-reading of the transcript some weeks later – after the pain and embarrassment had subsided somewhat – revealed some good data, but this wasn't an experience I wanted to repeat.

This leads us to consider the second facet of what we are calling collaborative awareness: the politics involved in gaining access to organizations, starting the project and developing a relationship with participants. We will not go into the procedures that are involved in gaining access to organizations in any depth: the reader may wish to consult a text such as Maylor and Blackmon (2005, pp. 268–272), who give a comprehensive account about using contacts and networks to secure access to a research site. We are more concerned here to argue that an appreciation of the political properties of establishing relationships with organizations and research participants, and indeed of research itself, is an important contributor to the researcher's critical consciousness. As discussed in Chapter 1, it cannot be assumed that all organizational gatekeepers of research will be sympathetic to giving access in the first place, and they may be especially suspicious of research approaches that entail using creative methods. The good news however is that it is just as likely that gatekeepers will be intrigued by the novelty of creative methods, and that this may result in a desire to know more – a potentially good platform for establishing a sound relationship with the fieldwork site. This is a reality that we

need to face from time to time. Many maintain that politics suffuse all social research (Guba and Lincoln, 1989; Punch, 1998) and this ranges from the micro-politics of relations with people in organizations through to the visible and invisible power of the system to put constraints, or not, on your research. Pam's and Mike's story illustrates the power of the system to either encourage or discourage support for a study.

Pam's and Mike's story

We may best introduce our initial experiences of the politics of gender research by outlining some of the discouraging messages we received. On some occasions we were discouraged by those who held reservations or who downplayed the potential importance of the study [a study of the experiences of women chief executives in UK local government]. It took us a long time to obtain funding from organizations that we regarded as obvious sources. We 'felt' the occasional covert disapproval coming from some of the power structures within the system. At times, it felt 'risky' to talk about the research. Not everybody was in favour of the research. Some of the more commonly expressed views included:

- There was no need for the study: women were being appointed in greater numbers and, in fact, you were now more likely to be appointed if you were a woman
- Such a study ran the risk of making women's experiences worse rather than better, by replacing old stereotypes with new ones
- Because the power-holders in local authorities are largely male, the study could alienate them and produce a 'male backlash'
- The experience of women is not substantially different from that of their male counterparts, and therefore there were no issues to be studied.

It was understandable that we would receive a mixture of expressions of both ardent support, but also of doubt and even hostility. For example, Pam was accused at one stage of being 'a bigoted old feminist' and Mike was sent a message that he had 'overstepped the mark'. However the expressions of encouragement far outweighed instances of negativity.

(Broussine and Fox, 2003, pp. 29–30)

Some of the political factors that have an impact on qualitative research in general, and fieldwork in particular, have been discussed by Punch (1998, pp. 162–166), who noted, incidentally, that these aspects have been under-discussed generally in research accounts. Consideration of these factors, including quite practical issues

that they throw up, would in themselves help to develop the researcher's critical consciousness, including a consideration of:

- Researcher personality – his or her approach, commitments, abilities
- Geographical proximity
- Nature of the research site, e.g. the organization
- Researcher's institutional background – may be of importance in trying to gain access
- Gatekeepers – the need to understand their needs, resources and roles
- Status of the researcher – age, ethnic background, gender.

Taking the last of these factors, Punch (1998) discusses how the race and/or gender of the researcher may preclude or open up access to research sites. On the one hand, he gives an account of a female researcher who failed to get into a masculine world (the policemen's locker room is cited). Similarly, another white, female, educated outsider found that her identity made it difficult to develop rapport and trust with research participants. On the other hand, Punch suggests (p. 165) a young student may be seen as less of a 'threat' than an older researcher.

Our purpose in outlining some of these anticipated problems is by no means to discourage the reader from contemplating the use of creative methods. Rather it is, again, to encourage and to suggest pointers that may help in the development of critical awareness that we are arguing is necessary in seeking access and developing relationships with people in organizations. Another way to see these factors, and the other aspects of critical awareness that we deal with in this chapter, is that these aspects need to be worked with even when access has been secured, and the study has begun. It would be naïve to assume, for example, that our gender, race, age and other aspects of identity will not affect our relationship with participants.

ETHICAL AWARENESS

We have learned that creative approaches suggest special ethical challenges. Brewerton and Millward (2001) provide a useful outline of the main ethical considerations that should apply to any management or organizational research. They discuss the dangers of involving people in research without their knowledge; of coercing participation; of withholding the true nature of research from participants; of deceiving participants; of leading participants into acts that diminish their self-respect; of exposing them to physical or psychological distress; of invading participants' privacy; and of withholding the potential benefits of the research from control groups (Brewerton and Millward, 2001, pp. 61–65). In addition, organizational researchers might be aware that the advent of 'research governance' in some institutional settings, for example, the UK public services, now demands a detailed knowledge of, and adherence to, ethical approval procedures (see 'Graham's Story' in Chapter 1, and

Department of Health, 2006). Whether on moral and/or legal grounds, researchers cannot ignore ethical considerations.

There are three ways in which we need to consider ethics as we use creative methods. The first concerns working with research participants' feelings, emotions, recollections, stories and personal experiences as empirical data. The second is to do with the vividness of the research experience for participants who produce drawings, work with poetry, stories, drama and dialogue in the inquiry. The third focuses on the need to withhold some information about the inquiry process from the prospective research participants in order to engage them spontaneously.

Turning to the first of these considerations, a question that the researcher might want to ask is: 'What right do I have to access participants' lived experience?' After all, it is conceivable that participants may reveal to the researcher (and to others like colleagues in a team and organizational setting) thoughts and feelings that they had up until then kept private, and perhaps not even admitted to themselves. The potential for harm or embarrassment is apparent. The data can be poignant, difficult and emotional. Of course, that is also the strength of creative methods, because they enable us to access data that sometimes lie deep in organizational settings. However, the potential power of the approaches obliges us to be ethically aware. One could imagine a nightmare scenario, in which the researcher, having elicited much data at some emotional cost to participants, leaves the site of inquiry with all the data captured, but the participants in a mess. The ethically aware, and collaborative, researcher will realize the importance of his or her obligations to participants in terms of initial clarity about the aims of the proposed study; promises of confidentiality and anonymity; assurances that individuals will not be identifiable in any reports of her study; choice about whether to take part or not; information about follow-up events; and opportunities for participants to see and amend draft accounts of the research and analyses of data.

Our second consideration concerns the potentially vivid nature of the experience of being researched through creative methods. In our experience, people who take part in research where they were asked to produce drawings which expressed their feelings; or where masks were employed; or where poetry was generated, can remember the experience in great detail some years later. The events, whether in inquiry groups, workshops or one-to-one encounters with the researcher, tend to be memorable. When we use creative methods, our relationship with research participants is likely to be intense – even intimate. In a positive sense, the vividness of the experience can shape their lives, because of the insights and learning that they may have gained from the experience. However, the potential negative side of this coin is that research participants remember the experience for quite different reasons – that they felt abandoned, betrayed, abused and manipulated.

Finally, we reach a knotty issue that applies to many of the creative methods that we deal with – that of asking participants to work spontaneously with us. This problem is particularly testing in collaborative forms of research. Of necessity, sometimes we

cannot be completely open with participants about the aims of the research or our method. For example, a research student of ours recently inquired into the psycho-dynamics of bullying in organizations. He wanted to examine the phenomenon not just from the victim's point of view, but as part of a systemic and complex set of relationships which included the alleged bullies. This necessitated interviewing the bully as well as the victim. It is apparent in this example that to have asked people outright why they bullied their staff would not be a viable option. Instead, he needed to approach the topic obliquely, not mentioning bullying at all, but giving the ostensible topic as 'organizational leadership'. It is important to add in this case that he had been open with senior representatives of the host organization, e.g. human resources directors, who understood and endorsed the approach. Punch (1998) gives another example – that of participant observation. Here the researcher may have to 'pose' as a member of a particular organization while not actually being one – having to act out a role. He reported his experience of conducting research as a participant observer with the Amsterdam police for six years, and concluded that this method necessarily entailed some secrecy. At the time he found 'all this genuinely distressing and confusing' (Punch, 1998, p. 178).

One of our assumptions is that subjective and personal data that are generated through spontaneous self-expression are valid. The degree of spontaneity will vary from project to project, and from method to method. For example, our experience is that the effectiveness of researching through the medium of drawings and art is enhanced when there is an element of participant surprise (we look at the implications of this in some detail in Chapter 4). The same is true of the use of masks (Chapter 7). Spontaneous expression, where required, asks the researcher to deliberately break a commonly accepted precept of ethical research mentioned earlier, that of not withholding the true nature of research process from participants. Partly, this question is to do with timing: there comes a point early in the encounter with research participants where the researcher will need to explain what is to be done; what process will be employed; and what their roles are in the process. However, if spontaneity is essential, then this briefing will happen only very shortly before one invites participation in the method. This requires preconditions of co-operation, respect and trust to have been generated between the researcher, participants and sponsoring organizations. Such a platform for implementation of the research will need to have been built earlier through the prior assurances and promises about the ethical treatment of research participants that we discussed above. In addition, however, there will be a need to be up-front (and ethical) about *not* telling participants what exactly will be demanded of them, and why. It is as well to be aware, however, that the advice that we have just given can be contested. Some researchers might consider that withholding *any* information about our research approaches is inimical to the proper treatment of research participants. So, in the end, as critically aware researchers, we are faced with dilemmas and choices, and these choices are at least partially to do with our political and moral stances. In such

dilemmas are contained both the difficulty and the fascination of carrying out creative organizational research.

CRITICAL AWARENESS AND VALIDITY IN WORKING WITH DATA

We now discuss some of the challenges and dilemmas involved in working with data that emerge from the use of creative methods. Each of the subsequent chapters will deal with the special properties of the data generated by the particular method covered. In one way or another, they all produce relatively unorthodox data and, taken together, a wide range of types of data such as drawings, poems, stories or metaphors is possible. They provide data sets of words, texts and symbols – the things that people have shared about their experiences of organizational life. The question arises about what meaning and validity can be ascribed to this data. Is it giving an insight into the authentic lived experience in the social system being investigated, or is it what the participant wants the researcher to hear? To a researcher who is concerned to access the underlying and sometimes unconscious meanings of what research participants communicate, these are critical questions. Coming to research from an interpretivist paradigm, the researcher will be curious to know what these words, texts and symbols mean. For example, what is revealed about the underlying unspoken principles that people hold (but maybe cannot articulate) about organizing; about power and gender relations; about the implicit rules that are operating; or about their roles? A big challenge facing us when we employ a creative approach to inquiry is to find ways of understanding what lies beneath the surface of what people communicate to us, while seeking to address our research question.

We will begin by tackling the issue of *validity* of data gained and interpreted through creative methods. The notion of validity here is quite different to scientific notions of validity that tend to rely on statistical tests. Here we are dealing with subjective accounts of lived experience, and the idea of validity is therefore more problematic. Questions of validity of qualitative methods generally apply to creative methods in organizational research, and Guba and Lincoln call paradigm differences about validity an 'extended controversy' (Guba and Lincoln, 2005, p. 205):

> Validity is not like objectivity. There are fairly strong theoretical, philo-
> sophical, and pragmatic rationales for examining the concept of objectivity
> and finding it wanting. Even within positivist frameworks it is viewed as
> conceptually flawed. But validity is a more irritating construct, one neither
> easily dismissed nor readily configured by new-paradigm practitioners.

Easterby-Smith *et al.* suggest that there is an underlying anxiety among researchers that their research will not stand up to outside scrutiny, and they show how notions of validity (and reliability and generalizability) vary considerably between different

research paradigms (Easterby-Smith *et al.*, 2004, pp. 52–53). Thus, they suggest that from a social constructionist point of view, *validity* is seen as the extent to which the study clearly gains access to the experiences of those in the research setting; *reliability* is seen as the extent to which there is transparency in how sense was made from the raw data; and *generalizability* is seen as the extent to which the concepts and constructs derived from the study have relevance to other settings. Such propositions add to the creative researcher's capacity for critical awareness in analysing and interpreting data. Nonetheless, it would not be surprising if the researcher was left with some anxiety of the type that Easterby-Smith *et al.* speak of, i.e. about being able to defend one's study in terms of its legitimacy and rigour, particularly when employing less-orthodox methods. We suggest that the critically aware researcher will not try to suppress this anxiety, but rather work with it as a means of remaining alert to crucial questions about the data that have emerged from one's study. We will return in Chapter 8 to questions about legitimacy and rigour, once we have completed our journey of learning about the range of creative methods in this book.

Our five forms of awareness that we are discussing in this chapter overlap to a considerable extent. A strong confirmation is made by advocates of collaborative forms of research for critical selfawareness or critical subjectivity, and crucially that this reflexive awareness is central to the processes of analysing and interpreting data and therefore to validity in collaborative approaches to inquiry (Reason and Rowan, 1981). For example we need to develop our capacities for noticing our 'unaware projections' – our ability to self-deceive – that can contaminate both the choice of methodology and the interpretation of data, by allowing one's own fears, defensiveness and biases to skew the research endeavour.

In addition to considerations of validity, the management and organizational researcher needs to wrestle with a dilemma about how he or she works with data. On the one hand we are interested in creative methods of research because they can enable the expression of participants' feelings and stories. Therefore our inclination is to want to allow this voice to be heard with little or no imposition of others' (including the researcher's) mediating influences or meanings. We are inclined, in other words, to let participants speak for themselves. On the other hand, the researcher is invariably challenged by results that contain a high degree of complexity, ambiguity and contradiction. Organizations are not the rational places that orthodox texts suggest, and we have to accept that we will need to organize our data in order to make sense of it. This dilemma itself invites the researcher to work in a critically aware way.

There is a range of available theories and ideas that suggest ways in which we can consider our data in all its contextual richness. For example, organizational psycho-analytical theory is centrally concerned with unconscious processes at work (see, for example, Gabriel, 1999), while organizational culture theory is concerned with sets of basic assumptions, norms and shared values held by organizational members (see, for example, Schein, 1992). Set alongside such theoretical frameworks – and this is less-good news if you want to look at it that way – the wide range of approaches to

data analysis can be bewildering. Denzin (1998) reviews a range of interpretive styles and practices, including grounded theory, constructivism, critical approaches, and post-structural interpretive styles. Each of these may be seen as lenses through which we might detect situated meanings that lie behind the drawings, poems, dialogue scripts, stories and metaphors that research participants share with us.

As the researcher works with data, he or she will need to hold an awareness that, while research participants may express a rich and multifaceted account of their lived experiences, these expressions are taking place in a context of which they are both part of and simultaneously creating, or enacting (Weick, 1979). Creative methods are inherently beguiling, and the data that they produce – drawings, stories, poems, tales, dramas – full of meaning. This is their power, but the researcher also needs to be sensitive to the situated nature of the data as indicative of individual and collective meanings beyond, behind and beneath the individual's or group's expression – through whatever method that has been used to enable that expression. In other words, the interpretivist paradigm in which these creative methods sit opens us to more understanding about social systems and people within them than we might at first imagine.

There is no one best way of analysing data that are gained using creative methods. We are attracted to Denzin's (1998) view that the interpretation of data is an *art* or *craft*, and that the qualitative researcher is invariably confronted by the difficult task of making sense of the data. With creative approaches, we may say that the researcher needs to make sense of participants' sense-making. The art that Denzin speaks of is that of the researcher as *bricoleur* (French for 'handyman', someone good with their hands), which derives from the French verb *bricoler* 'to do odd jobs', or 'to potter or tinker about'. In other words, the task of the researcher is to immerse her or himself in the data; work with the data inductively and reflexively; play and wrestle with the data; and seek useful meanings and categories. The researcher 'fashions meaning and interpretation out of ongoing experience' (Denzin, 1998, p. 315). Denzin and Lincoln (2005) have recently elaborated on the notion of the *bricoleur*. They argue that the qualitative researcher as *bricoleur* 'stitches together' (rather like a quilt-maker); or assembles images as a montage (rather like a film-maker); or blends different voices and sounds (rather like in jazz improvisation), in order to create representations of complex situations. This leads to the proposition that the qualitative researcher may utilize or develop methodological practices to suit the needs of particular inquiries. Thus:

> If the researcher needs to invent, or piece together, new tools and techniques, he or she will do so. Choices regarding which interpretive practices to employ are not necessarily made in advance. … These interpretive practices involve aesthetic issues, an aesthetic of representation that goes beyond the pragmatic or practical
>
> (Denzin and Lincoln, 2005, p. 4)

CONCLUSION

We have argued that effective use of creative methods in organizational or management research requires five critical 'awarenesses' – methodological, critical self-, collaborative, ethical, and data validity awareness. The cumulative effect of developing these types of awareness is to encourage the researcher in her or his task of developing what we described as a capacity for critical consciousness through the whole inquiry process. Research into people's lived experiences, narratives, emotions and recollections invariably generates an important by-product, that of learning about ourselves. We would go so far as to say that this self-learning is not just an incidental benefit of engaging in studies and inquiries of the kinds that we look at here; rather it is an intrinsic part of taking up our roles as creative organizational researchers with authority and integrity. The process of undertaking a challenging inquiry can be transformative, in that the development of critical consciousness in the process can frequently challenge our basic assumptions and values about knowledge, people, social systems and ourselves. In Chapters 3 to 7, we will show how the researcher may be creative in research. But the good thing about the approaches is that, along the way, we will learn about the phenomenon that will be of great interest to us – ourselves.

DISCUSSION QUESTIONS

1. Why is it important that the researcher has awareness of the philosophical (ontological and epistemological) bases of his or her proposed study?
2. Why is researcher reflexivity so important in the effective use of creative inquiry methods in organizational and management research?
3. Is all qualitative research political?
4. What are the special ethical considerations involved in creative approaches to organizational research?
5. How may creative methods be seen as seductive?

FURTHER READING

The Denzin and Lincoln (2005) handbook, together with Easterby-Smith *et al.*'s 2004 book are useful companions to this chapter (and book) in their different ways. For example, Guba and Lincoln's (2005) Chapter 8 in *The Sage Handbook of Qualitative Research* (Third edition) provides, among other analyses, an accessible problematization of the notion of validity in qualitative research (pp. 205–209). This chapter in the *Handbook* is one of 44 that deal with different aspects of

qualitative research, including discussions about research paradigms; methods of collecting and analysing empirical materials; and the art and practices of interpretation and presentation. The book is therefore a major tome, but the researcher will be rewarded by finding there a wide range of insights into the theoretical and practical challenges involved in qualitative research. Mark Easterby-Smith's and colleagues' introduction to management research provides the reader with an additional (and shorter!) resource that specifically addresses the needs of the management researcher 'who is actually doing some research' (Easterby-Smith *et al.*, 2004, p. xi), i.e. starting management research, designing it and doing it. They argue that 'management research is both more complex and more simple than is normally implied by the text books' (Easterby-Smith *et al.*, 2004, p. xi).

We have argued in this chapter how critical subjectivity and reflexivity are central to the researcher's capacity to employ creative methods effectively, and Kim Etherington's 2004 book provides a third accompanying text for the reader who wishes to go further into this important topic. The book represents the author's own journey, which is characterized by reflections on her own research and encounters with a range of other researchers' stories as they become reflexive researchers.

Denzin, N.K. and Lincoln, Y.S. (Eds) (2005) *The Sage Handbook of Qualitative Research* (Third edition), Thousand Oaks, CA: Sage Publications

Easterby-Smith, M., Thorpe, R. and Lowe, A. (2004) *Management Research – An Introduction*, London: Sage Publications

Etherington, K. (2004) *Becoming a Reflexive Researcher*, London: Jessica Kingsley Publishers

THE METHODS

CHAPTER 3

CREATIVE DIALOGUE

Mick Beeby and Peter Simpson

OVERVIEW

- Creative dialogue as a form of collective inquiry
- Underlying principles and theory
- How to use creative dialogue in organizational research – creative dialogue for a shared organizational problem, or dialogue in a collaborative research group
- Two case studies showing creative dialogue in practice
- Working with the data
- Conclusion
- Discussion questions
- Further reading

CREATIVE DIALOGUE AS A FORM OF COLLECTIVE INQUIRY

Alan took the creative dialogue method to a compound in Lusaka, Zambia, where three key people from different aid agencies had major difficulties with each other. This was threatening the future existence of the health project, affecting up to 80,000 people. Alan took his flipchart and spent the weekend with the three leaders, working together using a dialogue procedure to explore their shared problem. At a pivotal moment, one of the trio stood up and wrote, 'It's me – I'm the problem' on the flipchart. This moment of insight did not lead to a scapegoating of this one individual – on the contrary, it freed all three leaders to reinterpret their struggle,

not as a battle with each other, but as the challenge of finding constructive ways of working together. The three leaders have now put forward a proposal to their agencies, which has been accepted. Alan was ecstatic – 'It works!' he wrote in an airmail letter from the compound.

This is not a piece of research, but it is an event that arose from the use of dialogue as a research method. A friend of Alan's was participating in a collaborative research group using a dialogue method. She suggested to Alan that he might consider using the method to prepare for the task that he would face in his new role, where he would be involved in projects seeking to improve the lives of families hit by AIDS and HIV. Alan took up the offer, and so, on a sunny afternoon in a Devon garden, a group of friends and colleagues worked together to produce three learning maps that eventually travelled from a Devon back-garden to a shantytown compound in Zambia, where the process was successfully replicated.

By engaging in dialogue with others, Alan was able to explore his thoughts and feelings about his new role ahead of time, and to envision the inherent challenges and possibilities in ways that he had not previously considered. Our own experience had been similar when, in our collaborative research group, we experienced the power of dialogue to recreate meaning when new and shared understandings of issues and events seemed somehow to unfold from our public discussions. Dialogue creates a novel setting that changes the everyday ground-rules for interpersonal communication, and replaces these rules with prescribed roles and behaviours that determine who, when and how co-researchers will interact as storytellers, listeners and sometimes as flipchart 'artists'. In this way, unlike many other approaches, the procedure creatively incorporates multiple methods for accessing experiential data (for example, storytelling and artwork).

By way of explaining dialogue, we can start by asking whether the reader will remember occasions when she or he was in discussions with others about something in a group – a group of friends or colleagues, a meeting, tutorial or seminar for instance – and felt really frustrated. It might be productive to try to disentangle the possible causes of this frustration. Perhaps you felt you could not get a word in edgewise. Perhaps you noticed that someone else in the group could not find their voice. You thought at times that the discussion or argument was getting nowhere. Perhaps you were unimpressed by the ways that some people in the group dominated the discussion. And, ultimately, you felt that the discussion achieved nothing. These are the kinds of everyday experiences that we have where we know that there was something not right about the processes of engagement and communication between people.

What dialogue tries to do is to get underneath the causes of this kind of typically frustrating experience. Figure 3.1, lists the kinds of behaviours that are helpful to dialogue and therefore which can help us to address why meetings sometimes can be irritating experiences. We aim to show how this can be achieved in a research context.

1 Reliance on discussion, not speeches
Learning by talking – involves exchange of data, reasoning, questions and conclusions

2 Egalitarian participation
Equality: hierarchy is a great inhibitor of collective learning

3 Multiple perspectives
Differences foster collective learning – there is a need for a variety of perspectives to
    challenge accepted practice and to hold ensuing tension whilst new learning emerges

4 Non-expert-based dialogue
Organizational members thinking together have the capability to generate workable
    answers to the organizational problems and cannot act responsibly except on the basis
    of their own conclusions

5 Participant-generated database
Participants are the primary sources of data – public discussion constructs meaning

6 Creation of a shared experience
Provide a shared experience of acting in new ways

7 Creation of unpredictable outcomes
The meaning that the collective constructs is relatively unpredictable.

Figure 3.1 Critical Elements for the Facilitation of Dialogue (Adapted from Dixon, 1997)

Dialogue enables people who are trying to work together, like colleagues and/or co-researchers, to reveal, encounter and capture the nature, origins and consequences of sense-making processes in the 'here and now' of human interactions in organizations. Dialogue is collective inquiry into collective thinking and meaning-making processes that generates research outcomes in the form of collective learning. Collective learning can be viewed as a participant-generated database, as co-researchers are the primary sources of data from which their public discussions construct shared meanings.

Dialogue involves deliberately bringing to the surface the underlying assumptions and mindsets that govern people's individual and collective behaviour in social interactions. As with all of the creative research methods that are considered in this book, dialogue allows the researcher and research participants to access rich and multifaceted aspects of their lived experience in ways that may not normally be available. In this particular case, dialogue brings unconscious aspects of the participants' thinking and decision-making processes into conscious awareness.

In dialogue, personal and collective meanings may be said to 'vibrate', and are shaken around to reveal new understandings and action possibilities. It enables different 'ways of seeing' to unfold with regard to participants' reported experiences of, for example, their work roles, relationships, shared problems and significant events.

This can be liberating for individuals and teams as they come to realize that they can change what and how they think together as a means of attaining their visions and goals. Equally, this can be threatening to those who may be used to exercising power through their ability to impose their definitions of situations on others.

We have used dialogue successfully as a collaborative procedure for researching processes of organizational learning, strategic development and organizational culture change; group and team dynamics, with particular reference to decision making and problem solving; and leadership as a distributed process of reciprocal meaning-making (Beeby *et al.*, 2002). Dialogue can also be usefully integrated with the sense-making and action planning components of other interventionist forms of organizational inquiry such as action research and action learning. These approaches lend themselves to creative dialogue as they seek to implement organizational changes that are anchored in collaborative diagnoses of problem areas that typically involve the collection, discussion and interpretation of data as the basis for collective action.

As dialogue is a complex and elusive concept, we begin this chapter by considering alternative ways in which it has come to be defined and characterized in the literature. We then present two methods that we have used in our own research. We provide case-study examples of how we have used these methods in practice to collect, record and analyse experiential data.

UNDERLYING PRINCIPLES AND THEORY

Peter Reason (2006) has proposed that dialogue may be seen as central to action research, and as contributing to what he sees as the contemporary movement in qualitative research:

> ... away from validity criteria that mimic or parallel those of empiricist research toward a greater variety of validity considerations that include the practical, the political, and the moral; and away from validity as policing and legitimation toward a concern for validity as asking questions, stimulating dialogue, making us think about just what our research practices are grounded in, and thus what are the significant claims concerning quality we wish to make.
>
> (Reason, 2006, p. 191)

The concept of dialogue came to the fore in the literature on organizational learning and knowledge management during the 1990s, as a new type of communication process that is characterized by collective thinking (Beeby and Booth, 2000). Dialogue emerged as a special kind of talk that involves more than the familiar everyday communication processes of conversation, discussion and debate (Schein, 1993;

Watkins and Golembiewski, 1995; Dixon, 1998). It additionally embraces the thinking processes and patterns that underpin such transactions between people. In a seminal contribution to this field, Isaacs defines dialogue as 'a sustained collective inquiry into the processes, assumptions and certainties that compose everyday life' (Isaacs, 1993, p. 25) and reports its emergence as a 'process for transforming the quality of conversation' (Isaacs, 1993, p. 25) in group settings.

Schein states that 'an important goal of dialogue is to enable *the group* to reach a higher level of consciousness and creativity through the gradual creation of a shared set of meanings and a common thinking process' (Schein, 1993, p. 43). He argues that dialogue as 'a basic process for building common understanding' (Schein, 1993, p. 47) is a necessary condition for effective communication between members of different cultural subgroups, and thereby for tapping into the collective intelligence of disparate group members to enhance organizational learning.

Dixon (1997) uses the metaphor of *hallways* to locate dialogue as the second stage of a three-stage process of organizational learning. The metaphor represents the process by which individually held tacit and explicit meanings are made accessible to others and thereby become shared, collective meaning. Dixon's model is summarized in Figure 3.2.

In this metaphor, individuals working alone construct meaning from their experience in *private offices*. What is known by the individual remains private unless and until it is made accessible to others during meetings in *hallways*, where collective

Private Meaning (*Private Office*)	Accessible Meaning (*Hallways*)	Collective Meaning (*Storeroom*)
Meaning is constructed by individuals out of their experience.	Collective meaning is constructed among organizational members through dialogue.	Meaning is held in common by organizational members
Individuals hold both explicit and tacit meaning.	Only explicit meaning can be communicated to others, but, in the process, tacit meaning can be revealed.	Both explicit and tacit meaning are held in the storeroom: explicit meaning in documents and policies, and tacit meaning in the culture and actions of organization members.
What is known by the individual is not accessible to others.	What is known by individuals is made accessible to others.	Explicit meaning that is held in common is accessible; tacit meaning that is held in common is inaccessible.

Figure 3.2 Differences between Private Offices, Hallways and Storerooms (Adapted from Dixon, 1997)

meaning is constructed by organizational members through dialogue, and then held in common by them as if in a *storeroom*.

Dixon (1997) identifies learning maps as one of several *hallways* that are currently in use in the real world of organizations. By learning maps, she means 'graphic, wall size illustrations of an issue an organization is dealing with', around which learning occurs via team discussions that are characterized by seven critical elements. These are elements that 'any such process would need in order to facilitate collective meaning' through dialogue. The elements are listed in Figure 3.2.

Much of the literature on dialogue merely assumes its validity as a research tool, and focuses instead on its use in organizational interventions. Although this is clearly a strength of the method, and as such it may be located broadly within the field of action research, it is also worth situating it within the appropriate research literature before exploring particular research methods based on dialogue.

From the research perspective, Reason and Heron's articulation of co-operative inquiry may be viewed as an early description of dialogue as research. They describe co-operative inquiry as a methodology for research 'with persons', in which all those involved are co-researchers and co-subjects 'participating in the activity that is being researched' (Reason and Heron, 1986, p. 458). In co-operative inquiry (as in dialogue), research conclusions are 'rooted in and derived from the experiential and practical knowledge of the subjects of the inquiry' (Reason and Heron, 1986, p. 458), and generated by those involved in the experience of being researched.

In this model, co-operative inquiry alternates between action and reflection in four phases. At the outset, in *phase 1*, 'a group of co-researchers agree on an area for inquiry and identify some initial propositions', and 'may also agree to some set of procedures by which they will observe and record their own and each others experience' (Reason and Heron, 1986, p. 459). When under way *in phase 2*, 'the group then applies these ideas and procedures. They initiate the agreed actions and observe and record the outcomes of their own and each other's behaviour' (Reason and Heron, 1986, p. 460). *Phase 3* is fundamental to the inquiry. Here the co-researchers become fully immersed in the activity and experience, to the extent that 'at times they will be excited and carried away by it: at times they will be bored and alienated by it; at times they will forget they are involved in an inquiry project'(Reason and Heron, 1986, p. 460). However, during this phase they also may develop 'an openness to what is going on for them and their environment, which allows them to bracket off their prior beliefs and preconceptions and so see their experience in a new way' (Reason and Heron, 1986, p. 461). *Phase 4* of co-operative inquiry completes the cycle of action and reflection, as 'the co-researchers return to consider their original research propositions and hypotheses in the light of experience, modifying, reformulating and rejecting them' at which point 'they may also amend and develop their research procedures' (Reason and Heron, 1986, p. 461).

HOW TO USE CREATIVE DIALOGUE IN ORGANIZATIONAL RESEARCH

Creative dialogue is a group-based method of organizational research that generates data through processes of collective inquiry. There are many ways of approaching such an endeavour using the general principles outlined in the previous section. Here we will consider two approaches. The first is an approach for working with groups of individuals from the same organization who have a shared problem that they wish to inquire into. This approach draws considerably on the work of Isaacs (1993). The second involves the formation of a Collaborative Research Group (CRG) with members from a number of organizations. This is a development of Nancy Dixon's (1997) approach, incorporating an original mapping procedure.

Creative dialogue for a shared organizational problem

Isaacs (1993) developed a set of principles for taking a group into dialogue rather than discussion, and describes its use in bringing together organizational members who are in conflict situations (in particular, a case study of union-management conflict is presented). Such cases of extreme difficulty in collective activity expose clearly the differences of intention and conflicts of interest that exist between different individuals in all organizations. As a research method, the principles of dialogue are consequently ideal for accessing the rich and multifaceted differences between organizational members at the deep levels of intentionality and assumption. A dialogue inquiry can be set up based on any shared organizational problem where there is a sufficiently strong common desire to work co-operatively together and yet where the organizational group is failing to reach a resolution on the matter. Stuart's case study is a very good example of the type of issue that we are talking about.

Case Study: Stuart – a PhD student's story

I have a friend who is a trustee for a charity that works in some of the poorest areas of a UK city. Like many charities, they were finding that money was hard to come by. My involvement was triggered by an 'opportunity' to raise a significant amount of money through Lottery funding. Unfortunately for those who thought that this could be the answer to their dreams, there was a small but significant group who did not want to have anything to do with money that was raised from gambling. Their argument was that gambling addiction was one of the problems that affected a number of clients that this charity sought to support. It appeared that this group would rather the charity fail to survive than compromise its principles. I must admit, I could see where both sides were coming from.

Continued

My friend knew that my research involved working with teams on decision making in difficult situations, sometimes using dialogue as a method, and she asked me if I might be able to help. The charity could not afford to pay – 'but perhaps it might be useful for your research?' I agreed to meet with the whole decision-making body of the charity, which comprised eight full-time employees and four trustees.

My friend talked me through the situation in some depth – particularly the nature of the characters involved and key relationships/conflicts, as well as aspects of context, such as the organization's history. I gained the impression of a group that was genuinely concerned about the work that it was trying to do, but with different views about how this might be achieved. The strained relationships that existed were as a result of these tensions, rather than particularly issues of personality.

I planned a simple dialogue session to last 90 minutes, inquiring into the question: 'How can we take the work forward?' I began by briefly introducing myself, the aim for the session, and the proposal that we use the dialogue method. As no one had come across the method before, I asked the group if they were prepared to trust me that this would probably be a good process. They agreed. I then explained some of the principles that we were going to use – talking them through the following ideas, in the form of a handout.

Explaining dialogue

- Our ability to think and make good decisions is generally damaged by two things: false harmony and constant arguments. Both stop us thinking together
- Dialogue is the art of thinking together
- The intention in dialogue is to reach new understanding and in doing so to form a new basis from which to think and act
- We seek to uncover shared meanings that can help align our actions with our values
- Dialogue is a conversation in which people think together. You relax your grip on certainty and listen to the possibilities that emerge
- Dialogue is a conversation with a centre – not sides
- Dialogue attempts to bring about change at the source of our thoughts and feelings
- Dialogue requires people to work with their uncertainties. It is not about defending one's certainties.

There was some discussion of dialogue, and after checking that there were no more questions, I restated the question and handed the task over to the group. I then worked at staying silent, encouraging the group to allow me to let go of the leadership role that I had taken on in setting up the exercise. After a few questions, which I answered briefly, the group grasped the fact that it was down to them. I then worked hard at intervening rarely, and then only to gently remind the group of the principles of dialogue – particularly when disagreements and discussion (sometimes heated) began to develop.

I concentrated on note-taking, because I find that it helps me to track the pattern of contributions and the emerging meanings and issues as they develop. This also serves a research purpose, although I tend to place even greater emphasis on making field notes – both in preparation, before the event, and in reflection, after the event.

As always seems to occur, all of us were struck – and sometimes amazed – at how easily resolvable misunderstandings had developed between people, and that the positions people appeared to have taken were not actually as hard-and-fast as others had assumed. The Lottery issue was barely addressed as the group joined together in exploring 'how to take the work forward' – the dialogue method seemed to encourage a richer exploration of the complexities of the work and each individual's reasons for being involved. The emotional texture of the conversation was thick with meaning, as individuals expressed their thoughts and concerns for their clients, the origins of the work, and their hopes for the future.

Together we entered a different mental space. There was no panacea, but there was a quality of conversation that exposed some of the depths that ran beneath the individual and collective activity that characterized this organization.

Dialogue in a collaborative research group (CRG)

Dialogue can be a potent reflective process. For researchers, the reflexive dimension of dialogue is equally important, providing a process for exploring one's role as researcher in the research process. Consequently, when it is possible to engage participants as co-researchers, dialogue becomes particularly powerful as a research method.

We recently established a collaborative research group comprising academic researchers with co-researchers from organizations in the region. This group was set up as one of the outcomes of a conference that had created research groups 'in which academics and practitioners could work together to reflect on and inquire into major issues facing local government' using collaborative and action research methodologies. With a shared interest in the method, our group chose to inquire into the practice of dialogue, meeting every six weeks for a year.

We will now discuss how this group developed its collective inquiry, and will use Reason and Heron's (1986) four-phase framework to demonstrate the sequence of issues that the management researcher would need to address if he or she chose to adopt this approach.

Phase 1: co-researchers agree on an area of inquiry

At an early meeting of the CRG, we discussed and agreed our overall aim as follows:

> To develop members' individual and collective understandings of the theory and practice of dialogue and to evaluate its potential worth and practical utility as an improved means of communications in local government.

We subsequently formulated research questions to provide a more specific operational focus for the research in areas of particular interest to us. Our research questions were:

• What is dialogue?
• Can we make it easy and simple to apply?
• Will it work in our own organizations, and, if so, where?

Thus the research task that we had set ourselves was that of transforming the complex, multifaceted and abstract concept of dialogue into a practical, easy-to-use tool for enhancing the quality of communication in our organizations by means of co-operative inquiry methods.

Phase 1 (continued): co-researchers ... agree to some set of procedures by which they will observe and record

The group met regularly every six weeks, on ten occasions, for sessions that lasted three hours. Immediately following the conference, we agreed that we would individually re-engage with the literature on organizational learning in a search for a set of practical guidelines that might enable us to engage in dialogue quickly and easily.

Based on Dixon's discussion of the core notions of the hallways, critical elements for dialogue, and learning maps, we were able to devise and agree an integrative, original set of procedures by which we would observe and record our own and each other's experience. This process began with each member of the group taking a turn at presenting a case story. The procedure that we developed and adopted is summarized in Figure 3.3.

In this way, we applied Dixon's (1997) three-stage model of organizational learning as both a practical, procedural means of structuring the design of our subsequent dialogue sessions, and as an analytical tool for inquiring into and making sense of their content and processes.

Step 1, learning map 1 – the private office (personal learning)

- The storyteller provides an unscripted account from personal experience of an episode/incident that that s/he believes illustrates something of significance about communications in his/her organization
- As s/he tells the story, s/he maps the episode using artwork to create map 1 on a flipchart
- Other CRG members remain silent though attentive.

Step 2, learning map 2 – the hallway (collective learning)

- The storyteller remains silent
- CRG members continue to apply the initial guidelines in the process of creating a second piece of artwork, map 2, on a second flipchart
- In this stage, members speak when moved to do so, by publicly sharing any connections and/or intuitions and/or images that were triggered for them by the story as told and then recording these images in turn on map 2.

Step 3, learning map 3 – the storeroom (collective meaning)

- Using the two maps as visual prompts, all CRG members reflect together on stages 1 and 2
- This takes the form of a collective review of the learning that has occurred about dialogue from the process and content of the session that is then recorded as map 3.

Figure 3.3 The 'Three-Maps' Dialogure Procedure

Phase 2: the group then applies these ideas and procedures

We subsequently used the 'three-maps procedure' at five successive meetings of the group, at which a personal case-oriented approach was deliberately used to ground sessions in current organizational realities and to inform our evaluation of dialogue as a practical and helpful tool for application in organizational settings.

Session by session, each CRG member in turn told of personally significant episodes of organizational communications, whilst simultaneously creating a pictorial representation of their story on a flipchart (see, for example, Figure 3.4). In this way, we told each other stories about the personal effects of rumour-mongering; the politics of taking up a promotion; responding to a colleague's anger; the feelings aroused by a boss's departure; and power and influence in facilitation (i.e. private office, private meaning).

The listeners then created a second learning map containing images of the thoughts, associations and intuitions that had been triggered for them during the storytelling (i.e. hallway, accessible meaning, and dialogue), see Figure 3.5.

Finally, and for each story, a third learning map was produced by the storyteller and the listeners together. This recorded in writing the learning that emerged for all participants from a review of the process and content of the session (i.e. the storeroom, collective meaning), see Figure 3.6.

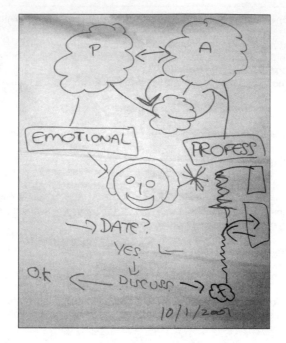

Figure 3.4   Example of Learning Map 1

Figure 3.5   Example of Learning Map 2

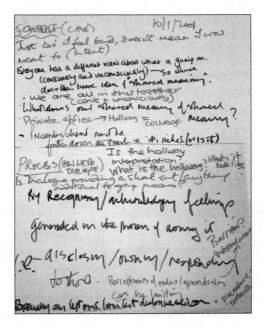

Figure 3.6   Example of Learning Map 3

Phase 3: co-researchers become fully immersed in the activity and experience

Each meeting of the research group was an intensely emotional experience. This was primarily due to the personal (often hurtful) significance of the organizational stories selected for telling, and the feelings that they aroused for the teller as she or he revisited difficult encounters and (re)presented these in picture form on a flipchart in front of co-researchers. At times, in response to hearing such stories, we abandoned the learning-maps procedure to counsel and support each other in relation to problems encountered in our other worlds 'as needs be' and as an emergent part of our practice. This provides an interesting element in our answer to our first research question – what is dialogue?

At other times, in other sessions, we laughed, cried, argued, confided, worried, disclosed, trusted, defended, accepted, disagreed, bonded, smiled, listened, owned (and owned up to), let go of, confronted, challenged, experimented, risked, worked, discovered, and learnt. In our individual and collective anxiety, the emotions of fear, guilt and anger were often to the fore. In part this answered our second research question – can we make it easy? – for although we had developed a procedure that we believed simplified some complex ideas, the emotional challenge of this work was not made easy at all.

WORKING WITH THE DATA

Whilst it is clearly possible to analyse the data from dialogue events in one's 'private office' as a lone researcher – and indeed this is necessary when participants do not wish to become co-researchers – we will consider here the process of analysing and interpreting research data whilst still engaged in the process of dialogue. This was the final phase of our CRG's research activity.

Phase 4: co-researchers return to consider their original research propositions

We have no doubt that in the example we are using here, all CRG members became fully engaged in the research process. This meant working with, against and around the research questions at different times, individually and collectively, during meetings, whilst moving in and out of (though always returning to) the three-map procedure.

We found learning maps to be a rich source of alternative perspectives on each of our stories, as told in line with Dixon's (1997) claim that because graphics are more ambiguous than words, the maps provide a focus for the discussion yet allow a wide range of ideas to emerge. Unlike when using word-based cognitive maps, the emergence of new and different meanings was graphically illustrated quite literally within the predominantly pictorial three-maps procedure. This occurred on five separate occasions when viewing map 1 (personal learning) alongside map 2 (collective learning) for the purposes of reviewing and recording our learning on map 3 (collective meaning). When compared with learning-map 1, learning-map 2 was often starkly different in tone and texture, and in the use of symbols, colours and shapes.

The differences between maps 1 (individual) and 2 (collective) may be viewed as the concrete and visible outcomes of a collective process of reality reconstruction that provided the storytellers in every case with an immediately accessible and visual alternative interpretation of personally significant events.

In our experience, in so far as each story revealed the storyteller's prior beliefs and preconceptions – and the learning maps also captured these – then these beliefs and preconceptions no longer need to limit or constrain individual learning. Group members were able to respond to individual mindsets, once these had been surfaced in story and picture forms, to produce collective and visible reconstructions of reported events that enabled each storyteller, should s/he choose, 'to see their experience in a new way' and to act differently.

At the CRG meeting that followed the sequence of five consecutive storytelling meetings, all the sets of learning maps were displayed together for the first time and reviewed in a reflective two-hour discussion. The discussion moved freely between the research questions, and also drew on members' experiences when testing the procedure in a range of organizational settings.

The discussion was tape-recorded and subsequently transcribed and content analysed by all members of the CRG collectively in open session. In this way, initial conclusions about the nature of dialogue and its relevance and application in local government settings were identified and agreed in line with the original research questions and aim.

CONCLUSION

This chapter has shown that creative dialogue approaches are methodologically 'rich', in that they provide the opportunity for co-researchers to use, in combination, a range of means of progressing their inquiry, including the use of art, storytelling and, of course, an application of the principles of dialogue. One of the challenges that we set ourselves in our exploration of dialogue that led to our adoption of the three-maps procedure was to simplify a complex process. Isaacs' principles of dialogue are to an extent straightforward. However, there is no doubt that a group-based research method that encourages participants to surface and work with deep feelings and assumptions will inevitably be complicated to manage at times.

This means that this approach has certain emotional risks attached to it for all involved that are, perhaps, as difficult to manage as some of the other methods that are explored in this book. For this reason, we would suggest that the organizational researcher seeks experience in dialogue events in relatively safe environments (such as working with experienced practitioners, or with a small group of colleagues), before launching into an event with virtual strangers (as Stuart did in his work with the charity). This is important, as we have a responsibility as researchers to help potential participants to make informed choices about engaging (or not) with procedures that can trigger deep-seated emotions such as fear, guilt and anger. A degree of experience on the part of the researcher is therefore required, unless the co-researchers are already skilled in group process work.

Potential limitations of the approach relate to the length of time required to develop sufficient trust between co-researchers to maximize openness in their exchanges. This is likely to be the case in research teams new to this approach and to each other, and these teams will also need to invest time in developing a shared understanding of dialogic principles and how to apply them in their interactions.

On balance, we see the need for a flexible and contingent implementation strategy that emphasizes different dimensions of a dialogue approach (for example, Dixon's hallways model and/or Isaacs' principles of dialogue and/or our own three-maps procedure) as judged appropriate or not for different groups by the researcher *in situ*.

Once a group is under way, the researcher's role is to intervene in timely and appropriate ways to ensure that the group's behaviour accords with the principles of effective dialogue. In particular, this will involve finding ways to slow down the group's collective urge to make decisions and to solve problems in response to a particular story, by asking them instead to share and record their feelings about what they had just heard, in line with the procedure. These are important procedural interventions that can also help to create a safe container for dialogue by holding the boundaries of the session.

The three-maps procedure outlined in this chapter is a valid, robust and easy-to-follow set of guidelines for doing dialogue in a way that accords with Reason and Rowan's characteristics of collective inquiry, as well as Isaacs' principles of dialogue and Dixon's (1997) critical elements. In our practice, for example, the process was *egalitarian*, in that each person in turn was a storyteller. Everyone also had a meeting allocated to their story. Although sessions varied, each took the form of a *discussion* in which ideas and other forms of *data* were *generated by group members* as we participated in a *shared experience* of storytelling and retelling, of drawing and redrawing pictures, and of collective sense and (non) sense-making.

DISCUSSION QUESTIONS

1. What is the distinction between a 'normal' work meeting and a creative dialogue, and why not use the former as a research tool instead of dialogue?
2. Why might participants in a creative dialogue resist the process?
3. How do you see the differences between dialogue and other processes for working with different viewpoints such as mediation, conciliation and arbitration?
4. Why would it be helpful for co-researchers' initial ideas about creative dialogue to be mapped at an early stage in the research process using the three-stage procedure discussed in this chapter?

FURTHER READING

Dixon's and Isaacs' articles, both published in *Organizational Dynamics* in the 1990s, are seminal outlines of the theory and practice of dialogue in organizational settings, and therefore represent important additional reading in support of learning from this chapter. Kemmis and McTaggart (2005) make the case that strategies for participant-driven and collaborative research, such as the approach outlined in this chapter, have their origins in resistance – particularly among participatory action researchers – to conventional research practices. Their chapter brings together the authors' earlier work, and provides a comprehensive survey of the nature of participatory action research (PAR), its origins and traditions, key features, the role of the facilitator in action research and the politics of PAR.

Dixon, N.M. (1997) 'The Hallways of Learning', *Organizational Dynamics*, Vol. 25, No. 4: 23–34

Isaacs, W.N. (1993) 'Taking Flight: Dialogue, Collective Thinking, and Organizational Learning', *Organizational Dynamics*, Vol. 22: 24–39

Kemmis, S. and McTaggart, R. (2005) 'Participatory Action Research: Communicative Action and the Public Sphere', in N.K. Denzin and Y.S. Lincoln (Eds) *The Sage Handbook of Qualitative Research*, London: Sage Publications, pp. 559–603

ACKNOWLEDGEMENT

Figure 3.2 and excerpts from Nancy Dixon 'The Hallways of Learning' in *Organizational Dynamics*, Vol. 25, No. 4: 23–24 reprinted with permission from the author.

CHAPTER 4

DRAWINGS AND ART

Mike Broussine

OVERVIEW

- **The power of drawings and art as a research method**
- **Underlying principles and theory**
- **Visual sociology and semiotics**
- **How to use drawings and art in organizational research**
- **Working with the data**
- **Conclusion**
- **Discussion questions**
- **Further reading**

The drawing in Figure 4.1 was one of 86 generated in a research programme that looked into the feelings of public service managers towards organizational change. The participant who drew this provocative and violent image was a member of a local authority chief-officer team in the UK. When he revealed his drawing to his colleagues on the team, there was a stunned silence. The senior manager told us that doing the drawing evoked anger in him about how 'we're being screwed by government at the moment', and he was surprised by what he had drawn. The devil represented for him a destructive and spiteful central government, the decapitated maiden the vulnerable local authority, and on the back of this drawing he wrote: 'Power at any cost (Government)/Lost touch with the real world/Dogma and ignorance/Make all local government suffer/Not interested in facts only prejudice/ We are only mortals doing our best/Struggle to retain some pride and quality of service/Not much to fight with/In limbo'. The drawing – clearly a *cri de coeur* – communicates something of the anger felt by many senior managers about the

Figure 4.1 'The Decapitation'

Figure 4.2 'Destruction'

perceived dysfunctional central- and local-government relations. The process, he said, allowed him to access his hitherto unspoken feelings, and he was glad to get them off his chest. He was able to 'say the unsaid'. A colleague in the same board contributed the drawing in Figure 4.2.

Such images, and the dialogue they provoked in the team afterwards, communicated real anger towards the 'perpetrators' of change, combined with a foreboding about their own and their organizations' futures. The senior local government officer who drew this image wrote on the back of his drawing, 'hostility, unenlightened, chaos, spite, double standards', capturing, for him, the characteristics of those who had caused such destructive pressures, i.e. central government (Vince and Broussine, 1996).

From these examples, the organizational or management researcher who is interested potentially in using drawings and art as a research method may realize how asking research participants to produce art – whether drawings, painting or collage – enables us to learn what is going on for them in their organizations and roles; their lived experience; their emotions and anxieties; and what is preoccupying them. The usefulness of drawings and art as a research method derives from the immediacy of expression; from the emotions that they capture or evoke; and from the fact that drawings may give us insight into unconscious as well as conscious thoughts and feelings. This chapter will explain how to use drawings and art as a research method in a critically aware way in order to access such data.

Russ's story

One member of a departmental team that I recently worked with drew a picture of his team as a boat, a pleasure cruiser. The Head of Department was on the top deck, staring to the horizon; the Deputy Director was lying on a sunbed on the middle deck; the other team members were doing various on-board tasks; and the manager who did the picture was leaning out of the back of the boat with an egg-whisk trying to make it go (Vince, 1995, p. 11).

UNDERLYING PRINCIPLES AND THEORY

Stiles (2004, p. 127) has wondered why, given the 'qualitative power' of images, researchers have been reluctant to use the pictorial form as a way of researching. In an echo of our earlier discussion about the position that positivism still holds in research, he suggests that people can experience a difficulty in accepting the subjectivity that is inherent in this and, we might say, the other methods covered in this book. Images can be thought of as being difficult to interpret and to categorize. He adds that the use of images in research can be regarded as unorthodox, inferior or eccentric. We have also found that the use of drawings and art can be thought by some to be legitimate as 'tools' for use in management development and by consultants running team-building away-days, but they hold less legitimacy for some as organizational research methods.

However, as Stiles (2004) and Mullen (2003) have noted, there has been a growth in the use of drawings and other arts- and metaphor-based approaches as recognized research methods, particularly where interpretivist approaches have been adopted to explore feelings, emotions and lived experience. In fact, the employment of drawings and art as research methods in organizational and management research became noticeable from the mid-1980s and 1990s. For example, Zuboff (1988) asked clerical workers to draw pictures showing how they felt about their jobs before and after the installation of a new computer system. Zuboff felt that the drawings acted as a catalyst to help staff articulate implicit and hard-to-define feelings. Meyer (1991) explored the use of visual data (drawings in particular) in organizational research, and offered a variety of insights, including the propositions that drawings are capable of communicating information about multidimensional organizational attributes; that the use of drawings as a research method is based in an assumption that research participants often possess more complex, subtle and useful cognitive maps of their organizations than they can verbalize; that the integration of visual data with verbal data may be a very useful form of triangulation; that drawings often prompt active participation in the research enterprise; and that visual data can enhance the capacity of research participants to make sense of, and attribute meaning to, events and experiences. Meyer continued by emphasizing the need for the researcher to work with participants, while holding an assumption that the research endeavour is a participative and collaborative one in which the researcher does not impose interpretations or meanings:

> Visual instruments seem uniquely suited to situations where a researcher aspires to some precision in measurement, but prefers not to force informants into his or her cognitive framework prematurely. Such occasions include investigations of amorphous concepts, efforts to build theory, and research focusing on human awareness, interpretation and consciousness.
>
> (Meyer, 1991, p. 232)

While we are not offering an authoritative art history lesson here, an acquaintance with the aesthetic philosophy of *expressionism* provides some insight into what lies at the heart of this creative method. Expressionism is an approach to the creative arts in which an artist, poet, dramatist or writer sets out to express an intense inner emotional experience rather than to attempt to depict impressions of the external world (Behr, 1999). Expressionists do not seek to portray objective reality, but rather the subjective emotional responses that objects and events arouse. Edvard Munch and Franz Kafka could be said to be expressionists, as could Vincent Van Gogh and Bertolt Brecht. Unlike the impressionists, expressionists did not set out to reproduce the impression suggested by the surrounding world. Instead they sought to impose their own feelings about what a particular reality provoked in them. The search for harmony and realistic forms was less important than expressing an intensity of emotional expression. As we saw in Chapter 1, and as an iconic example, Munch's painting *The Scream* shows this intensity.

It would be misleading to regard expressionism as a unified philosophy with a cohesive style, but the term emerged in the late 1890s, according to Behr (1999), to depict new trends in French art. However, expressionism in the visual arts and literature grew as a form of social protest, a pessimistic reaction to materialism, militarism, mechanization and urbanization in the late nineteenth and early twentieth centuries, particularly in pre-1914 Germany. Later the Nazis branded expressionist works as degenerate. Many expressionists went into exile, especially to the United States. However, expressionism went on to find new forms thereafter. Jackson Pollock's abstract expressionism, for example, represents a more modern form.

The use of art and drawings in organizational research has its origins in art therapy. According to Susan Hogan (2001) the term *art therapy* was first coined in 1942 by an artist called Adrian Hill, although she shows that therapy using image-making was carried out before this date. As Hogan explains, art therapy has many roots, but there are two precursors that we want to mention. The first is *expressive therapy* (or sometimes *expressive art therapy*) which Rogers (2001) locates in a humanistic and person-centred tradition that has been reserved for non-verbal and/or metaphorical expression (Rogers, 2000, p. 163). William Reich (1897–1957) is credited with bringing therapy and expressionism together before the Second World War (Reich, 1945). Reich argued that the repression of emotional energy could cause physical and psychological illnesses. In particular, he argued that repression lay at the heart of fascism and authoritarianism. The second root of art therapy was provided by Carl Jung (1875–1961), and this led to another precursor within a range of traditions and theoretical bases, that of *Jungian analytical art therapy* (see Edwards, 2001). Jung (1964) emphasized the importance of 'primordial' images and symbols as means through which we can tap into our unconscious. Images or pictures come through to us in dreams and fantasy. Psychological difficulties may be discovered through the interpretation of pictures as well as of dreams.

While we have briefly introduced these precursors as a contribution to understanding the underlying theory for the use of art as an organizational research method, it is important to know that there is a range of theoretical frameworks in which art therapy was and is practised, and the reader is recommended to consult both Susan Hogan's (2001) and Judith Rubin's (2001) books to gain detailed explorations about art therapy.

Liebmann (2004) maintained that the power of drawings is enhanced by the fact that they approach a person's and a team's unconscious feelings – a function which is confirmed by literature in the art therapy field. This is underpinned by a belief that clients may self-express in situations where it is hard to put feelings into words. Art therapy, she argued, uses art as a means of personal expression to communicate feelings rather than aiming at aesthetically pleasing endproducts to be judged by external standards. Liebmann, as well as discussing the history of art therapy, outlined in the rest of her book several processes which employ the use of drawings in group therapy situations. She thought that the group setting for art therapy held advantages over the individual approach, e.g. much social learning is achieved in groups; people with similar needs can provide mutual support; group members can learn from feedback; and groups can be catalysts for developing latent abilities.

While the method that we are outlining here is sometimes called 'art therapy', it would be a mistake to see it as such. Qualified art therapists in the UK undertake a two-year postgraduate diploma, and many are also qualified psychotherapists or psychoanalysts. The UK National Health Service is the main employer of art therapists in Britain, and art therapy invariably takes place within a clinical setting. But art therapy does provide a theoretical and practice basis for the use of drawing and art in organizational and management research. It is best to regard the research approach as one that owes much to art therapy, but our outline of the methods and the types of data that are gained is not intended to be used for therapeutic purposes.

Morgan (1986, 2006) is particularly credited with showing how insightful metaphor can be for analysing and understanding organizations. The reader may have experienced the use of art in her or his education, and may have been asked to 'draw your organization'. The purpose of such an exercise is to enable business or management students to visualize the concept of 'organization'. Many managers start by portraying 'organization' as a formal hierarchical structure. But they can also produce unusual, even whimsical, drawings, for example the organization as an amoeba, as medieval castle, or as a maze – each metaphorically representing their 'organization-in-the-mind'. Whatever images are produced, they convey how people feel about their experiences of organizations in ways which can communicate more than words are able to.

As we have seen, drawings and art in social research can give access to a person's or a group's unconscious feelings. The approach is underpinned by a belief that research participants may self-express in situations where it may be hard to put feelings or recollections into words. We are not looking for high artistic ability on the part of participants. Indeed, the paintings and drawings that can result can be messy and enigmatic. The point is that this messiness, if that is what emerges, may be communicating something about the originator's messy feelings or recollections. On the other hand, really neat and tidy images may be communicating clarity, or, alternatively, obsessive feelings, about the subject.

The theoretical approach that has been outlined may be described as one based in art psychotherapy. However, there exists a range of additional approaches and complementary frames with which the researcher might wish to acquaint him or herself. We will focus on two of these – visual sociology and semiotics.

Visual sociology

Harper (1998, p.130) described visual sociology as a subfield within qualitative sociology – 'the recording, analysis, and communication of social life through photographs, film and video'. He suggested that the approach originated in anthropology and is related to visual ethnography, and he advocated visual sociology as providing a model for collaboration in research and as an adjunct to the interview. Harper's chapter provides a comprehensive theoretical and historical commentary on the approach. Both Harper, and, more recently, Harrison (2002), have commented on the relative absence of the use of visual material – they refer to the invisibility of the visible, and the 'sightlessness' of sociologists – in social science research. Thus, Harrison, citing some other visual sociologists (Fyfe and Law, 1988; Chaplin, 1994) said that she:

> ... found this absence surprising: not only because of the ubiquity of visual images encountered on a day-to-day basis in a wide variety of social contexts; but also because we use visual skills and visual resources as 'taken-for-granted' ways of being in the world, even if such visual dimensions may be translated into words. In addition, much of the routine work of social actors in many different contexts requires visualisation as a component of human thinking and problem solving.
>
> (Harrison, 2002, p. 857)

In this approach, photographs (or film) can either be taken by the researcher or by participants. As an example, Harper (1998) shows how photographs taken by the researcher and which capture something that is culturally meaningful to the participant, are used to guide and stimulate dialogue between the researcher and interviewee ('photo elicitation'). In another mode, Harper mentioned that participants could direct the making of photographs before interpreting them in interviews – an approach carried out by Dutch students in a study of a neighbourhood. There is a range of ways in which such ideas could be adapted and extended (Riley and Manias, 2003). For example, the researcher could provide a wide range of postcards or similar images, either in a research workshop or inquiry group context or as part of a one-to-one interview. Each participant may be asked to choose (say) three that hold some meaning for them in relation to the topic being addressed. Alternatively, participants in an inquiry workshop may be invited to bring copies of published art and images that hold some meaning for them in relation to the research topic. Harrison (2002) critically reviews a range of visual sociology methods that may be used in the ethnographic and sociological study of health and illness, for example, film-making, photography, the creation of visual narratives using video cameras (in one case by children and adolescents who shared the medical condition of asthma), using both collaborative and participative research designs. Riley and Manias (2003) report on their Australian ethnographic study that examined the governance of operating room nursing using photography. They warn about a major ethical issue in the use of photography, in that this method can be highly intrusive, and report that securing ethical approval was not straightforward in their case. However, their study proceeded: participants were supplied with a disposable camera and asked to take photographs that showed 'the daily life of an operating room nurse', taken during the course of their everyday work routines (p. 84), and their article continues by discussing how such visual data may be analysed.

Semiotics

Moriarty (2004, p. 227) states that semiotics is the study of signs and codes – signs that are used in producing, conveying, and interpreting messages and the codes that govern their use. In semiotic theory, a sign is anything that stands for something else, so a sign stands for an object or concept (p. 228). Moriarty provides an overview of the theoretical work undertaken by Ferdinand de Saussure (1966), a Swiss linguist, and of Charles Peirce (1931), an American philosopher who developed a model concerning how reality is represented in thought and mind. She explains that de Saussure explored the relationship between the object (like a tree) and how the object may be signified, for example through words, pictures and gestures. Peirce, also working in the early twentieth century, thought that reality (and thoughts) can only be known through representation via signs; further that this signifying activity can best be explained through a three-part model of sign, interpretant and object. Moriarty argues that because of Peirce's emphasis on representation as a key element in how a sign 'stands for' its object, semiotics has become particularly useful to visual communication scholars 'who are, by definition, scholars and students of representation' (Moriarty, 2004, p. 229).

Semiotic theory is complex, and our purpose here is not to provide in-depth understanding, but rather, as with visual sociology above, to introduce the reader to additional possibilities for framing the use and interpretation of visual empirical material like art and drawings. The researcher may be attracted to pursuing a deeper understanding of semiotics, because it could provide a theoretical framework and additional means of accessing the connotations and denotations that are conveyed in images. Figure 4.3, from our own research, referred to earlier, provides an example of an image that signifies considerable meaning.

In this drawing, 'the building' certainly *denotes* a physical structure (which is being destroyed), but we might suppose that the manager who provided this image did

Figure 4.3 'Destroying What I Believe In'

not wish to convey a literal building, but rather a *connotation* or symbol of something more emotional and painful (as indicated by the title that he gave to his drawing). As Moriarty (2004, pp. 233–234) says:

> a photo of a house's elaborately carved wooden door may evoke not only an entry (the denotative meaning), but also wealth and art … – that is, people who can afford to own such an elaborate door probably live in fancy houses and appreciate 'good' art. Perhaps it also symbolizes the door to such aspirations … for people who dream of such a lifestyle with all its attendant symbols and associations – fancy car, Rolex watch, designer clothes, servants, travel, and so on.

Thus, the use of art as a research approach enables people to communicate multifaceted information and feelings about their experiences in organizations and other social settings. It legitimizes the expression of complex, subtle and possibly irrational facets of organizational experience. This may be important within certain settings, where it is 'not done' to give voice to feelings and irrational aspects of life. The methods also enable the integration of visual with verbal data. This is because the production of images by whatever means is not usually the be-all-and-end-all of the research. It is the dialogue, reflection and sense-making that is provoked in an individual or in a group by the production of expressive images that can be as important as the images themselves. We gained an initial insight into the procedures that we might employ to achieve this in Chapter 3. The production of art is engaging and 'hands-on'. However, the processes that we will outline are not for everybody: some research participants can be reluctant to engage with the process, but in our experience this happens only occasionally. Finally, the approach is particularly suited to the researcher who, working from an interpretivist perspective, does not want to impose his or her analytical framework on research participants, but rather to encourage them to be spontaneous and creative in their expression.

HOW TO USE DRAWINGS AND ART IN ORGANIZATIONAL RESEARCH

The approach comprises a range of methods, each of which in some way uses artistic expression. The first one, which we will mention most in this chapter, is asking research participants to produce a drawing using paper and pens or crayons. The reason for this is that the process is the easiest to set up: it does not, for example, need the researcher to carry paint pots around. Secondly, the researcher may need to consider how she or he might reproduce images in the eventual research report or dissertation, and ease of scanning may be important to keep in mind.

However, there are other methods within this approach that might be preferred. Choice of method will be informed both by the research aims or questions, but also by the researcher, as *bricoleur* (see Chapter 2), using an intuitive sense of what is most appropriate in the circumstances. The researcher's own liking for a particular medium may come into play, and this is quite appropriate, as the researcher maintains his or her critical self- and methodological awareness. Instead of participant-generated drawings, paints or other materials could be supplied for the creation of collages, for example tape, coloured paper, images cut out from magazines, and so on. There is another dimension of choice of method using drawings and art, that is whether the researcher wants images to be produced in the first instance by individuals, or by groups or pairs of research participants in a co-operative way. For example, a project's research aims may be concerned with discovering feelings about 'team effectiveness'. In this case, the researcher might be as interested in observing and analysing group processes as the images are produced through a team painting or collectively generated collage. Alternatively, the interest may be to examine the subjective experience of 'inter-personal collaboration'. In this case, the researcher might ask participants to work in pairs, sitting at either side of a small table, each with a set of crayons or paints, to produce a drawing or painting together. He or she might ask them to perform this task in silence, but, on completion, ask the participants to reflect on the experience that they have just had. This discussion will form an important part of the data.

A PhD student's story – Jenni

Great, but ... how do I use drawings? At a practical level what do I do? What materials do I use? What if the participants refuse to draw? How long should I allow? What do I do with drawings in the session once they've been drawn? How do I analyse them? This mixture of excitement and fear of using a more creative method was my initial feeling about using drawings as a research tool. As a result – and to allay my own fears of using a research tool that was new to me – I felt it was important to understand my own reasoning as a researcher why I wanted to use drawings and what value I felt they would add to my research.

The case in which I was contemplating using drawings was within a focus group of six people, where I had previously interviewed three of the participants individually in relation to the research topic. I wanted to use drawings with this group for three reasons:

1. To give all members of the focus group *a shared experience and a shared reference point* for the subsequent discussion of their thoughts and feelings around the topic of enquiry of the research.

Continued

2. To *centre the group's conversation* within the arena of the focus group and reduce the desire of those that I had interviewed outside of the focus group to refer explicitly to their individual interview in order to emphasize their point.

3. To gain *access to internal data* that otherwise may not surface in a group discussion due to the rawness of discussing individual emotions and feelings. Thus, I felt that the use of drawings might create a 'safe' outlet for participants to express their feelings to a depth that I suspected would be difficult to reach just in a group discussion.

Additionally, but no less important, I wanted to use drawings to introduce a 'lightness' to the concept of academic research, and to create a relaxed environment for subsequent discussion.

I did use drawings with this focus group, for all of the above reasons. However, their use provided much more. Drawings catapulted the group straight into discussion of the research topic, and were a useful tool through which to pull the group back to topic when the conversation wandered off track. The drawings (or process of drawing) seemed to create some sort of discursive synergy within the group, an 'X factor' that I don't think would have happened otherwise.

Given the necessary permissions for access, we are required to return to an ethical question that was discussed in general terms in Chapter 2. It will be remembered that one of the underlying principles of creative methods in organizational and management research is that that subjective and personal data that are generated through spontaneous self-expression are valid. The question arises therefore about whether or not research participants are to be informed in advance that they going to be asked to produce drawings or paintings. Associated with this question is the fear, as Jenni contemplated in her story, that all or some of them might refuse to co-operate. There is no definitive answer to this dilemma, and there is no point in pretending that this research method is risk-free. On the one hand, ethically aware researchers will not wish to manipulate the research participants, but instead to wish to work transparently. On the other hand, this approach relies on participants being able to voice feelings and experience through spontaneous expression, and this might be jeopardized were participants to know beforehand that they were going to be asked to produce drawings or other forms of art. Our judgement is that it is better to ask participants to produce their art with no prior preparation but, importantly, within the context that great care has been taken in the establishment of an appropriate collaborative researcher–participant relationship (again as emphasized in Chapter 2) at both the stage where access is sought to research participants, and at the stage when the researcher eventually meets them. The level of researcher–participant trust is therefore an essential factor at this stage, along with a clearly negotiated agreement with them to be prepared to go with the process.

In order to suggest a procedure, we will set up a scenario. The following outline is based on our research referred to earlier. This produced the 86 drawings by public service managers, concerning their feelings about organizational change. There is no suggestion here that the following represents *the* way to do it, but rather it may be regarded as a guide which the researcher may want to adapt to suit her or his purposes. He or she may want to adopt a completely different design, for example to ask individuals to work in pairs, or to ask a group to generate art-based data. Amanda's case study below suggests yet another approach. The working assumptions here, however, are that the researcher will want to rely on drawings as the medium of expression; that she or he will wish to invite individuals to produce them and that participants will have the opportunity to offer their first interpretations of them; that this is taking place in a group or workshop context; and that the aim is for the drawings to act as a catalyst for group analysis and dialogue, which will need to be recorded in some way.

In this study, the researcher took with him some A3 paper, felt-tip pens for the drawings, and a tape recorder. Each workshop group consisted of six to eight participants and lasted about two hours. In this illustration there are four stages of procedure, each introduced by the researcher with a task brief:

1. Asking research participants to produce a drawing – 10 minutes
2. Inviting them to reflect individually on their drawings – 10 minutes
3. Whole-group work – showing and discussion of each drawing in turn – 80 minutes, i.e. approximately 10 minutes per drawing
4. Review – 20 minutes.

'1) For the first stage please draw – on your own – a picture or image using the resources provided which expresses your feelings about change at work in your organization. Try not to use words if you can possibly help it. You're not going to be evaluated on artistic ability - for example matchstick people are fine. Pictures only have to be complicated in so far as your feelings are complicated.'

This first stage does not need to take long – perhaps ten minutes at the most. Once participants think for a moment about the brief and the topic, a mental image often emerges quite quickly. The researcher will be prepared for surprise on the part of participants, and be prepared also for expressions of anxiety, for example, 'But I can't draw.' We will return to this kind of anxiety later. Reassurance may need to be given, emphasizing that this is not an art competition. Sometimes it helps – if someone is really stuck – to sit alongside him or her and ask open facilitative questions, such as, 'When you think of ... , what sort of image comes into your mind?'

2) 'Secondly, after drawing your picture, reflect on it for a few minutes: then write down on the back of your picture words or short phrases which come to mind when you look at your picture'.

In this way, the first interpretations of the drawings are carried out by the research participants themselves, before any further interaction between members of the group.

3) 'Thirdly, I invite you to work as a whole group. In this phase, each participant in turn is asked to show her or his drawing. We will spend a few minutes looking at each drawing. When your drawing is on display, it is interesting to remain silent while others in the group offer interpretations and meanings that your drawing evokes in them. Once this has been completed, you will be invited to comment on your own drawing. The procedure continues by repeating this process with the other drawings'.

What lies behind this part of our procedure? We have found that it is important to honour and give attention to each individual's efforts in turn, and to legitimize the expression of what it may have felt unsafe to say. Originators of drawings can find this part of the process intriguing, because colleagues in the group may suggest meanings that they had never meant to convey, or did not know that they had conveyed. Further, the researcher will be just as interested in people's meanings and interpretations in the dialogue that is collectively provoked by the drawings, and the recording of this discussion and underlying discourse will, in this design, form a central part of the empirical data, along with the drawings themselves. We have already seen (Chapter 3) how drawings can be used within creative dialogue in a group inquiry.

4) 'Finally, the group's task is to review what has come out of the inquiry. This is the last part of the process for today'.

This last phase enables the researcher, with participants, to pull the threads together. It is worth asking participants about their feelings regarding what has emerged from their workshop, their learning, and what they felt about the process itself. This discussion may also form part of the data, and also contributes to a critical reflection on the research methodology.

The critically aware researcher will realize that this process can make some participants confront some difficult feelings or recall painful experiences. The significance that this holds for research participants should not be underestimated, particularly as after having filled the blank sheet with their feelings, the researcher may be asking them to disclose their drawings and what they represent to colleagues. Research participants can experience a range of feelings about being asked to

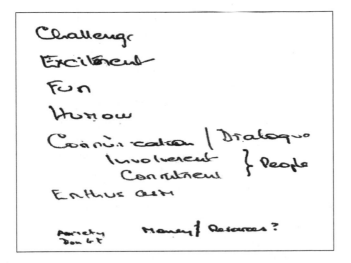

Figure 4.4 'The Reluctant Drawing'

produce a drawing or other form of art. There is likely to be some initial anxiety and surprise. However, there can also be a sense of being involved in something novel and intriguing. It is rare that participants refuse to co-operate altogether. Out of the 86 managers in our study, only one refused. He could not produce a drawing as such, but he agreed to set down a series of words. Here was the result (Figure 4.4).

This 'image' was still useful. Compare the sizes of the words used in the middle with those that the manager has squeezed in at the foot of the piece of paper. The subsequent discussion about what he produced was illuminating for colleagues in his team (who had all produced drawings), because the manager revealed that he felt he had denied difficult feelings that he had not felt able to explore or express to himself. This example emphasizes two things. Firstly, it points to the importance of working with emotion that is not only conveyed by imagery, but also that which is created when being asked to participate in the process itself. Secondly, it reminds us that people have a right to refuse if they want to. This may cause embarrassment and difficulty, but if the researcher holds an ethical stance on this, refusal does not necessarily mean that there will be no learning.

WORKING WITH THE DATA

What kind of data does the approach generate? What is the balance between images and words? And who is interpreting the images? We have already mentioned that the artwork – whether drawings, paintings, or collages – that might be generated is only one form of data that the approach gives rise to, crucial though it is. The other forms of data are the interpretations of the drawings or paintings. Researchers can sometimes make the mistake of thinking that it is they, and they alone, who should carry out the interpretation of the images. Certainly, their analysis of the images will be an important component of their study, but, working within an interpretivist paradigm, the researcher will want to access the range of possible constructions and meanings that people place upon their subjective experiences as represented, in this case, through their drawings or paintings. Research participants' involvement in this process may be regarded as an 'unlocking' process through which they may be able to voice feelings or recollections in ways in which they might otherwise have been unable to do. If we take this view, enabling participants to offer interpretations and reflections on what has been produced becomes central to the approach.

The process of dialogue and discussion that is stimulated and guided by the procedure is as important as the art itself, as are the feelings among research participants about being asked to participate in the process in the first place. They will have undertaken their own interpretations, and they will have engaged in dialogue with others about the issues that have emerged for them. The dialogue will be recorded in some way, e.g. by a tape recorder supplemented by the researcher's field notes, and this dialogue itself constitutes important empirical data. In this case, the researcher will have access to a multilayered set of data which cumulatively will yield a rich sense of what is going on in that group or organizational context, and in the individual participants themselves (see Figure 4.10). Nonetheless, the production of images is a critical beginning of the data-gathering process, and the researcher will wish to work with the art produced, and set his or her interpretations alongside those of research participants. In this section, drawing partly on Furth (1998) we will suggest some typical patterns that may appear in the art that can guide your interpretations. Before that, Amanda's case study shows how one organizational researcher did it.

Case Study: Amanda – an MBA student's experience

'Then' and 'now' drawings were completed as part of an away-day with the project team in a clinic which formed part of the student's inquiry. Eight pairs of drawings were completed, but, as an illustration of my interpretive approach, two pairs are shown here. Each member of the group was asked to draw a picture of how it felt to be working in the clinic six months ago, and then to draw another picture of what it felt like now. A sample of research participants' and my interpretations follow each pair of 'then' and 'now' drawing (Figures 4.5 and 4.6).

Figure 4.5   First Pair of 'Then' and 'Now' Drawings

The research participant said in relation to the 'before' (left) drawing in Figure 4.5: *'My feelings show that the majority of staff were all in high care awaiting yet another crisis to happen. One nurse out on the unit looking after 32 patients, answering telephones, answering doctors requests and the inpatients getting very little input – this resulted in all staff extremely stressed out.'* She outlined the feelings evoked by the right-hand ('now') drawing in these terms: *'This shows a lot more joint working between staff and patients and respect for each other. 'High Care' now feels that there is some control and therapeutic input. It now feels that staff no longer need to be in the office and this is now unstaffed. The whole unit now feels that there is less crisis working.'* My commentary was: *'The two pictures show a contrast between the 'anger and tension' in the nurses' faces in picture one and the relative calm in picture two. The strong barriers between parts of the clinic have come down, and staff and patients are together.'*

The meanings evoked in the 'then' drawing in Figure 4.6 were: *'Pressure on nursing, staff/patients confusion, nil organisation in management, nursing or medical undermined and overworked, 2nd class service, nil multi-disciplinary working and a poor public image … poor communication between management, medical, nursing and team with individual opinions and personalities carrying the load.'* As to the 'now' drawing on the right: *'Two-way communication, consistency, hard work will get results … pride in work … barriers broken, sharing the strengths and weakness … clarity … release of pressure'.* My interpretive comments: *'These two pictures are very 'busy' with lots of movement depicted by arrows and lots of hard barriers (black lines separating the doctors in their boxes at the top as well as the lines separating the unit from the rest of the service).*

Continued

Figure 4.6   Second Pair of 'Then' and 'Now' Drawings

> *The feeling engendered in the picture on the left is one of chaos, despair (nurses wailing), isolation and fear. The drawing on the right, although exuding more calm and control, with some of the barriers breaking down (e.g. the doctors), still seems quite isolating and anxious. However the colours are brighter and there are pathways and open doors into the clinic which indicates an opening up of process and feelings'* (Hedley, 1997).

In using drawings and art in organizational research, we have learned that the first pointer to guide the researcher's interpretations is to develop confidence about her or his own first impressions about the meanings being conveyed by the picture. Often, though not always, the expression is vivid, metaphorical and symbolic, and, as suggested earlier, much can be gleaned quite rapidly. The researcher is able to 'let the image talk' and having an overall feeling about what it is conveying can be seen as a fundamental part of data analysis, as is of course the participant's own interpretations of his or her drawing. The process can enable us to access data that are often good at revealing the emotional experience connecting an individual, the team, and the organization. Different parts of a drawing or painting may convey different aspects of lived experience and of emotions, and the images generated by individuals in a group may stimulate particular emotions in other team members.

It is not possible to predict what images will come out of this approach. Indeed it would be a pity if we could, because that would suggest that we can name and assign boundaries to people's expressive capacity. However, in addition to the overall feel communicated by an individual's or a group's art, there is a range of specific features that can emerge from the procedure.

'People' will often feature as images in drawings or paintings. We may be able to read the expressions that research participants may have put on their faces, as Amanda did. In our research, many of the drawings portrayed organizational life by using walls, sheep pens, fences, and, as the most extreme statements of separateness and defensiveness, castles and drawbridges (e.g. see Figure 4.7).

In some of the images, there can be items that, unexpectedly, are missing. On one occasion, a management team member completely forgot to include a team member in her drawing. In another piece of research, an image contained several people who had no eyes. The researcher needs to be prepared to accept that these omissions could be attributed to an accident of drawing or painting. However, when working with unconscious processes in individuals, groups and organizations, it may be fruitful to consider that such forgetfulness may hold some deeper meaning. The size of a part of an image can indicate either the importance, or the devaluing of, the person or thing that has been included in the picture. Where there is an anxiety about financial stringency in an organization, for example, there is sometimes a preoccupation with large or small currency signs. Generally, the distortion of shapes may symbolically portray problematic areas about the subject being drawn or painted. Hatred of

Figure 4.7   Castles and Drawbridges

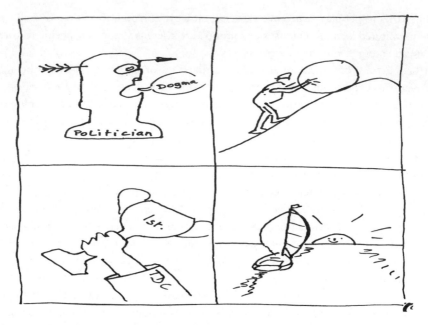

Figure 4.8   Hatred, Struggle, Success, Enjoyment

individuals or a class of people might be portrayed by grotesque or exaggeratedly ugly caricatures, as in the top left-hand quadrant of Figure 4.8. This drawing also shows another visual metaphor that may be generated to represent the feeling of being trapped in fruitless struggle – the myth of Sisyphus (shown in the top right-hand quadrant of this drawing).

The number of repetitions of a symbol in a drawing or painting may hold significance, of scale and importance. It is also worth looking out for the energy that has been invested in the shading of objects. On a number of occasions in our research, managers invested a lot of black ink in the depiction of heavy clouds, and this was invariably used as a metaphorical device to communicate anxiety, danger or looming threats. Edging or boxing in items suggests separateness from the remainder of the image, and can be used to convey a feeling of an individual or unit being beleaguered or disconnected from other parts of the organization.

Sometimes participants include clubs, swords, daggers or hammers in the hands of the people that they portray. The decapitation drawing in Figure 4.1 is a good example of this. Weapons can be seen as conveying the power or aggressiveness of the individuals brandishing them. Semiotic theory can aid our interpretations. For instance, it is worth noting that the participant may attach a special significance to the choice of weapon shown. For example, daggers may be closely associated with the notion of stabbing someone in the back, a particular connotation of experiences of the politics of organizational life.

Images can include some form of movement, progress, or transport. Managers in our earlier research used movement in a number of ways. Organizational change was often seen as a journey, and the choice of imagery suggested different feelings – for example, a cart being pulled through slow winding lanes into the sunset, as compared with an express train hurtling into a tunnel. In another form of movement, the trajectory of arrows can indicate conflict with, or aggression towards, the item (usually a human figure) at which the arrow would end up.

Trees can be used as a metaphor that contains a range of states of being. On the one hand, it may be that the conscious or unconscious employment of this symbol conveys balance, rootedness, health and 'one-ness' with the world. Some managers participating in our research drew poor, withered specimens of trees, images that might suggest the opposite, that is a feeling of the absence of the positive qualities of health, rootedness and so on. Abstract images can be difficult to fathom, and maybe that is their point. The participant's own interpretations may be of assistance here. Sometimes what is being expressed is something that the participant finds hard to understand, or it is ethereal or spiritual. Another possible interpretation of some abstract images may be that the person is avoiding something.

Finally, we may be able to offer an interpretation of a drawing or painting by, as it were, standing back from it, to see whether there is any significance about the way in which available space has been used. To what extent is the space on the paper filled in or empty? Where much blank space is left, this could indicate that the person is psychologically lacking in the energy required to 'complete' the picture: the topic may be too painful or difficult. On the other hand, a very crowded drawing in which complete use has been made of the space may indicate someone with a high fascination with the subject, or someone whose energy is overflowing. In the case shown in Figure 4.9, the expenditure of high energy and experience of 'busy-ness' by this participant has led to collapse and illness.

To summarize, the key to analysing the data coming out of drawings and art is to recognize two of its qualities – its multifaceted nature, and its metaphorical and symbolic character. Using something like the method that we have outlined results in data at multiple levels or ways of knowing, as depicted in Figure 4.10.

CONCLUSION

The reliability of drawings and art in a qualitative research process depends on an acceptance that recollections of lived experience, anxieties, and preoccupations can be expressed and contained (consciously or unconsciously) within an image. We also argue that, because this method, like the others in this book, invariably takes place within an organizational setting, drawings and art can give rise to intra- and inter-personal dialogues which together may be seen as a collective expression of context-specific discourses. The procedure that is suggested, which may be adapted to suit different research intentions, can generate a multilayered set of data, including:

Figure 4.9   'Busy-ness' Leading to Collapse

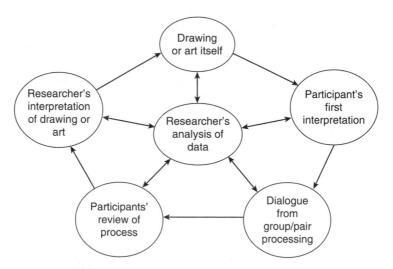

Figure 4.10   The Multifaceted Nature of Data from Drawings and Art

the drawings or art themselves, individuals' own interpretations of their images; the dialogue between research participants that is stimulated by the process of producing the art, and by the art itself; the feelings among participants about being asked to produce a drawing or painting; and, finally, your own interpretations and meanings that you put on the images (as summarized in Figure 4.10 above). The spontaneity of the process of generating drawings and art can give rise to a rich and diverse imagery representing a range of sentiments about organizational experience.

DISCUSSION QUESTIONS

1. How would you defend and explain the 'qualitative power' of drawings (Stiles, 2004) and similar arts-based research methods?
2. What ethical challenges are involved in the use of art and drawings as a method in organizational and management research?
3. Why may the data emerging from art or drawings be seen as 'multifaceted'?
4. How would you represent your personal experience of, and the emotions generated in, the process of undertaking research in a drawing?

FURTHER READING

As emphasized in this chapter, the use of drawings and art as a research method in organizational and management research does not constitute art therapy as such, but the origins of the approach owe much to the field of art therapy. The books by Hogan, Liebmann and Rubin offer the reader a more in-depth analysis of the history, theory and practice of art therapy. For a comprehensive introduction to the history, meanings and diversity of cultural practices that are manifestations of expressionism, the reader can consult Shulamith Behr's text. This short book (just 80 pages) includes many examples of expressionist art and photographs, and offers an accessible and lively account of what the author calls one of the great but most elusive '-isms' of the twentieth century.

Behr, S. (1999) *Expressionism*, Cambridge: Cambridge University Press
Hogan, S. (2001) *Healing Arts – The History of Art Therapy*, London: Jessica Kingsley Publishers
Liebmann, M. (2004) *Art Therapy for Groups – A Handbook of Themes, Games and Exercises*, London: Brunner-Routledge
Rubin, J.A. (Ed.) (2001) *Approaches to Art Therapy – Theory and Technique*, New York: Brunner-Routledge

ACKNOWLEDGEMENT

Text box on page 86 reprinted with permission from Amanda Hedley (1997) *The Emperor's New Clothes*, University of the West of England MBA Dissertation.

CHAPTER 5

STORIES

Peter Simpson

OVERVIEW

- **Stories as central to sense-making processes in organisations**
- **Underlying principles and theory**
- **Methods of eliciting stories – the interview, group work**
- **Working with the data – two case studies: analysing the structure of stories, working with paradox**
- **Conclusion**
- **Discussion questions**
- **Further reading**

The following is a brief excerpt from a research interview with Nicholas, the lead negotiator in a large Western multinational[1]. Nicholas is in the middle of a story about the early stages of an international joint venture, and, as you will see at this point, things were not going well:

Nicholas: 'the Russian negotiator was being particularly stubborn and I said, 'Mikhail this is ridiculous'. He looked at me and said, 'What do you know …?'

Researcher [interrupting]: 'Ouch!'

Nicholas: 'Yes, Ouch! 'What do you know? You know nothing. You don't know me, and you don't know these people – me and the Chinese. I do.' And he was right. I suddenly realised, 'I don't know you, obviously, and I don't know the Chinese, obviously.' Because he had years of experience, he had even been out there with them on aid programmes, as had the translator it turned out. But there was an anger in him there, it showed in his eyes, a real anger, and I thought I had really blown that one. So I stopped my tirade with him at that point and just backed off, and left it'.

The beauty of such a story for the researcher is that it captures an organisational experience with such richness of feeling and detail – a reality if you like – that can be seen in the interview and felt, even in reading the text. The experience is relived in retelling the story. The audience is allowed to experience it vicariously.

In research terms, this provides data that are particularly appropriate for the investigation of experiential phenomena. Contrast this with, for example, the sort of response that might be obtained if the negotiator was asked to complete a questionnaire or to 'outline the five most important elements of a successful negotiation in an international joint venture'. Karl Weick (1979) makes a similar contrast between the study of a fish, preserved and mounted and amenable to observation, with one on the end of a line, fighting for its life as the fisherman seeks to land it. The former provides observational data, the second experiential data.

In this chapter we are going to explore the practice of using stories in organisational and management research. Our starting point is that stories are central to processes of sense-making within organisations. Boje described storytelling as 'the preferred sense-making currency of human relationships' (Boje, 1991, p. 106). As a result, most people learn the art of storytelling, and the researcher of stories will not find it hard to gain access to good data. Provided that she or he does not ask questions in a 'factual' way, but rather gives people opportunities to 'talk normally' about the interesting aspects of research participants' experience, people will readily provide stories.

What we do in this chapter is to explore some research methods that can help to elicit stories. However, before we do, we think it only fair to let you know what happened to poor Nicholas. Had he really blown it? Would Mikhail ever forgive him? Would the joint venture fail? The story has not yet ended (so even we do not know whether the joint venture will finally succeed), but it did continue, and something changed:

> I don't know where along the line that it happened. He [the Russian negotiator] had a birthday dinner one night in Beijing. I got there late and when I arrived he had saved a place for me at the table next to him. All the heads of the delegations were at his birthday dinner, and he stood up and just gave this toast, 'And Nicholas, he's my best friend. I know that whenever there's a fight he's going to be standing right there behind me. That's what I know'.

UNDERLYING PRINCIPLES AND THEORY

The use of stories in organisational research has its origins in two literatures – the first on folklore, anthropology and myth, and the second in narrative analysis.

In the first, the focus of attention is upon stories that take on the quality of a 'myth', which persist within a particular culture and are told and retold time and time again. Such stories will be told at particular times, such as the induction of new staff, or in critical moments when the story provides some sort of explanation for the situation. While such stories persist because they embody something of general significance, it is important to recognise that the meaning of such stories will also change with the intentions of the teller and the listeners, and in relation to events that are unfolding. Consequently, research drawing upon this literature will tend to give attention to the meaning of a story in relation to the particular event.

The work of Levi-Strauss (1963) has been particularly influential in organisational research from an anthropological approach. The importance of mythical stories is their capacity to contribute to the resolution of life contradictions, with stories at an unconscious level helping individuals to bring order and understanding to their experience. In recent decades, the increasing attention given to change and uncertainty has led studies to draw upon the mythical quality of organisational stories in this sense-making process. We can see this in the mainstream culture-change literature (for example, Peters and Waterman, 1982) as well as the more academic studies of story and myth in the leadership of change (for example, Mitroff and Kilmann, 1975). A research design adopting such an approach will tend to focus on gathering stories that are frequently retold and play a particular role within an organisational culture (for an outline of such an approach see Gabriel, 1999, pp. 270–272). However, our focus here is on gathering stories that are constructed by the research participant as a part of the process of sense-making in the moment, as the storyteller works actively with the researcher. Such an approach draws more heavily on the second body of literature from which organisational research into stories has developed – narrative analysis.

Narrative analysis (see, for example, Labov and Waletzky, 1967; Labov, 1972; Bruner, 1990; Cortazzi, 1993; Riessman, 1993; Czarniawska, 1998, 1999) is concerned with the interpretation of communications, paying particular attention to a critique of the coherence and fidelity of the narrative, and with an emphasis on links with values, reasons, decisions and actions. Stories play a particular role in narrative analysis to the extent that they contribute to the continual creation and re-creation of our understanding of our place in the world. The important stories, from this perspective, are not those that exist and persist within a culture, but are our own stories and those that we are involved in creating with others.

Stories formed in everyday conversation, which may include those generated in research processes, are directly linked to the experience of organisational members and their desire to account for and make sense of their lives. Such stories are more personal, more immediate, and will tend to be told relatively infrequently, having a currency for a time but then being replaced by more recent stories that are relevant to current experience. Our focus with this form of story is on the manner in which individuals use narrative forms to work with their unfolding values and reasons, and subsequently to make decisions and take action.

The process of describing and working with experience in storied form is not without its complications – not least because words are not experience. As a researcher of such stories, we must therefore give attention both to the characteristics of the experience being described and to the nature of the language being employed. Extremely helpful in this regard is Clandinin and Connelly's understanding of stories as a 'middle ground' between experiences and the discourses (the body of language and meanings) that are available within a particular culture. They suggested that when people think and talk about their experience they do so in 'storied form', and they do not just record experience over time. Thus, a story has 'a sense of being full, a sense of coming out of a personal and social history' (Clandinin and Connelly, 1994, p. 415).

The challenge, from this perspective, is to adopt a research approach that will encourage research participants to tell stories that genuinely reflect their values and reasons, making sense of their decisions and actions. It is to this task of eliciting data in storied form that we now turn.

METHODS OF ELICITING STORIES

There are many ways to elicit stories from research participants. The most common is the interview, but there are many other approaches that may be adopted that can lead to rich and interesting data. We will first consider the interview method, and then look at a group-based method. In all cases, wherever possible, we record and then transcribe the conversations.

The interview

It is important to distinguish between different approaches to the interview, which can be used to meet different purposes, seeking different forms of data. Gabriel (2000) suggests that:

> it is necessary to distinguish between description, which deals with facts-as-information, and stories, which represent facts-as-experience...
>
> (Gabriel, 2000, p. 27)

The positivist approach to the research interview seeks to elicit 'facts-as-information'. The interviewer may, for example, ask for biographical details, or even specific questions about beliefs, feelings, motives, reasons or behaviour. The aim of such an interview is to generate data which will be valid as knowledge independent of both the research setting and the researcher or interviewer. For this reason, such interviews tend to be tightly structured, asking the same questions in the same sequence in the same manner.

In seeking to research data in the form of stories – 'facts-as-experience' – we might apply some of these principles to the interview, but our general approach will be quite different. For example, we tend to use storied data to investigate particular themes, and so will have a semi-structured interview approach designed to elicit particular types of story (e.g. 'your darkest moment as a leader' or 'a situation where you did not know what you were doing'). We have also found it helpful to seek some contextual information (e.g. a brief career history) as 'factual' material within which to locate the analysis of the stories. Jenni's story gives a good insight into this approach.

A PhD student's story – Jenni

I stumbled into the use of stories in my research. I didn't make a conscious decision to elicit stories – the interviewees just gave them to me, and when I started looking at the transcripts I was really struck by the number of stories that the interviewees told me. I think the reason that I got so many stories was the exploratory nature of the interviews, which were partially directive, and used only one main question: 'what is your emotional experience of remote working?'

As the interviewer, I worked throughout the interview at actively listening for emergent themes, and then asked the participant to 'tell me more about …' This approach allowed the interviewee to say what they wanted to in relation to the research topic in a way that they wanted to say it. Informal post-interview feedback that I have received from interviewees is that they likened the interview experience to having a counselling session, after which they felt 'less stressed' about their job.

The nature of asking people to talk about their experiences is explicitly linked to their feelings and emotions. Thus, the interview has the potential to turn into a quasi-counselling session, especially when people use a story as a way of voicing an emotive view and reliving an experience that they may perceive as negative. Although the use of open-ended questions allowed access to a mass of rich data, I found I had to work very hard at ensuring that I didn't 'open up a can of worms' and leave the interviewee troubled by themes explored in the interview process.

The stories that the interviewees handed to me in this piece of research added a real richness and depth to the data. Some of the stories were scene-setting, and allowed me a context in which to understand what the interviewee was trying to tell me. Other stories were used to highlight or make a point about the research topic; most were historical. However, one was very recent and obviously still uppermost in the interviewee's mind and emotional realm. It was here that I had to consider the interviewee's emotional welfare over and above the merits of gaining data for research, so I allowed the interviewee to tell me what she wanted to but didn't probe in depth into an obviously emotionally difficult story.

Within a loosely containing structure, which may bear some similarities to an interview that is seeking 'facts-as-information', our primary purpose is to elicit authentic accounts of subjective experience, and our practice is generally to move beyond 'asking questions' and seek to reach a state of 'engaging in conversation'. As an interviewer, a successful interview will involve becoming lost in the conversation, fully engaged – not somehow 'detached' as 'researcher'. At times, in the role of interviewer, one becomes aware of the need to reflect on such things as the time or whether other questions need to be asked. Provided, however, that one is clear on the purpose of the interview and that this has been adequately understood by the interviewee, little overt effort needs to be given to such issues, other than the normal processes of active listening (Rutter, 2003).

For example, as a group of colleagues we are currently engaged in a long-term project investigating 'what leaders do'. In these interviews we begin by requesting a brief career history, focusing on 'key moments' or events, and then focus on eliciting stories on our theme by asking about what they have done in 'good' and 'bad' times. In this design we are employing a version of the 'critical incident technique' (Chell, 2004), which can lead to very rich stories, because the 'critical' nature of the experience means that interviewees tend to have vivid recall of both events and emotions.

The interviews tend to last between 45 and 90 minutes, although they are sometimes longer, depending upon the time available and the desire of the interviewee to talk. We use an interview structure, outlining possible questions (Figure 5.1), which is sent to the interviewee prior to the interview. The focus is on the first three elements – career history, successes and tough times. The other questions are really there only as an *aide-mémoire* of questions and themes that we have found relevant in the past – issues that may be worth pursuing in the conversation as it develops. Once the early stages of the interview are passed, and the interviewee understands that the requirement is for a factual biographical account leading on to a series of stories about particular experiences, the interview structure can be

---

Leadership interviews: question planning

This is a selection of potential questions and areas for exploration. Not all of these are to be used.

- **Career history**
Please can you provide us with a brief overview of your career history?

- **Events and situations**
What were the most perilous moments in your career?
– how did you sense the danger?
Can you think of a situation in which your back was up against the wall?
– what did it feel like?
– what were the consequences for other people?
What are the three biggest successes of your career?
– can we focus on one of these?
What are the three most memorable events in your business career?
– can we focus on one of these?

- **Personal characteristics**
What are your strengths and weaknesses?

- **Leadership**
What are the most difficult and/or challenging aspects of leadership?
What do you enjoy most about leadership?

- **Philosophy**
Do you have what you might call a 'philosophy of business'?
What are your core business values?

- **People**
Who have been the key people working with you?
What is it about these people that you really valued?
Have there been any individuals who have had a particularly formative impact on your understanding of leadership?

Figure 5.1   Outline of Possible Interview Questions

left behind. As interviewer, it is important to have a clear enough sense of the issues worth pursuing, so that any notes or pieces of paper can be put aside to allow the conversation to take its course.

The intention is to allow the interviewee to enter that state of mind in which sense-making is taking place: we are not looking for 'packaged' memories or 'interesting stories', but to access the experience of the interviewee as fully as possible. The attention of the researcher and the interviewee must be – as fully as possible – on the experience itself. The interviewee should be allowed to experience the time again, to relive it in the retelling of the story. It is evident that inappropriate or overly frequent questions, or too much direction, from the researcher will prevent the teller from reaching this state. The researcher merely seeks to communicate genuine interest in the experience. For example, in the story excerpt at the beginning of this chapter, when the researcher uttered a spontaneous 'Ouch' in response to hearing about

Mikhail's attack upon Nicholas, we see an empathetic entering into the feelings as well as the facts of the story.

Group work on live stories

Another method that we have used successfully to elicit organisational stories involves working with groups on current issues requiring active attention. It works equally well with members from a single organisation or from a range of organisations. This group-based method is a form of action research (Eden and Huxham, 1996) that seeks to address live organisational issues in real time, providing a context within which the participants will gain insight and learning. While we are careful not to suggest that problems will be solved through the process – in fact we set up a process to explicitly avoid this – it is possible to be confident that the participants will find the experience valuable and rewarding.

This approach can increase the chances of gaining access to organisations over a protracted period of time, because it is possible to 'sell' the potential benefits that participants may gain from taking part in the process. This helps to gain a research relationship that allows stories to be explored as they unfold over time. One of the difficulties with the interview approach is that it tends to involve a single engagement with each interviewee, and demands a certain generosity of spirit from the interviewees prepared to give their time, often with little obvious benefit to themselves.

One particular approach that we have used with a number of organisations provides up to six participants with the opportunity to share a specific experience of taking up their leadership role in a 'live' situation within their organisation where they do not know what to do. In Figure 5.2, a number of the general principles concerning this method are set out. These notes were sent to the participants prior to the first meeting, as part of the negotiation process asking them to take part in the research.

The intention, as with the interviews, is to set up a containing process that allows researcher and participants to enter into real conversations. In order to achieve this, the process must be set up with a level of simplicity and clarity that allows the researcher to manage the process with minimal effort. It is important to ensure that the participants know what is going on at any point and what their role is in the research process. The general principles of the research are introduced and explained:

1. the nature of the *process* (bringing 'live' case studies to be worked on by the group) and the *theme* of the research;
2. the dual aims are outlined, in this case providing an opportunity for participants to 'explore and learn' (probably of greatest interest to the participants) and to conduct a research project (probably of greatest interest to the researcher);
3. clear objectives are articulated that are of value in relation to both of the aims – and therefore of interest to both participants and researcher(s);

Explanatory note – group research into leading in difficult situations

This process is intended to provide the opportunity to share a specific experience of taking up your leadership role in a difficult situation within your organisation.

Aim

To offer the members of the members of the Research Group the opportunity to explore and learn from their shared and different perceptions and experiences of working in role in the context of this leadership research project.

Objectives
To enable us to:

- gain insight into relationships and patterns of behaviour in situations of uncertainty;
- explore the ways in which personal thoughts and feelings can be managed in a leadership setting;
- explore strategies which might increase effectiveness in leadership roles.

The way of working

We will meet five times, on a monthly basis. Sessions will be two hours long. The basic material for sessions 2, 3 and 4 will be provided by case-study material based on the experience of two members of the Research Group taking up a leadership role in a difficult situation. In session 1, we will agree the sessions at which different participants will make their presentations. In session 5, we will review our insights and learning from the process.

By 'case study', we mean some kind of event, incident or situation that is facing you at work. It could be a recurrent problem or a one-off; it might be a 30-second interaction or involve a long-standing working relationship; it could be a clearly identifiable issue or one 'event' or meeting that left you feeling confused; it might involve several others or one person, and they might be at any level or any part of the organisation.

In preparing your 'presentation', you should think of a specific case – rather than something general, like 'managing people' – and it should be current – in other words something on which you will have to take action. This is not intended as a competition to see who can do the best presentation or prove that they are coping better than anyone else! Instead, the 'presentation' can be as structured/unstructured as you wish – and should in any case only last five to 10 minutes. It will help to choose an incident, event or situation that has aspects which are puzzling to you – either in how you find yourself reacting or in how other people behave – and where you feel that you need to understand more about what is going on before you can act.

The research project leader will manage the process. Each case study will have 45 minutes, to cover:

(1) brief presentation, followed by questions for clarification only (5–10 minutes);
(2) time for the presenter to sit back and listen, while the rest of us talk through what we think may be going on, in terms of the role of the presenter (15–20 minutes);
(3) time for the presenter to join in the discussion (15–20 minutes).

At the end of each session we will leave time for all of us to see whether there are any patterns emerging about the experience of the leadership role.

Figure 5.2   An Example of Eliciting Organisational Stories in a Group Setting

4. the way of working is outlined in some detail, clarifying the nature of
the commitment being entered into and including the respective roles of
participants and researcher(s).

A very important feature of this approach is that group members are encouraged
not to attempt to 'solve' the problem, but to make connections to their own
experience. The researcher's role as 'facilitator' of this collaborative process is crucial
at this stage, because groups tend to enter 'problem-solving' mode. Two features
of the approach are generally enough to inhibit this tendency. Firstly, once the
'case' has been presented and questions for clarification answered, the presenter 'sits
out' for the first part (10–15 minutes) of the group discussion (in this respect, the
reader will notice a parallel process suggested to facilitate a creative dialogue session
as discussed in Chapter 3, the 'three-maps' dialogue procedure). In combination
with this procedure, the researcher reminds the group with a phrase such as: 'the
problem does not need to be solved by the group: all we need to do is to make
connections with our own experience. In fact, the presenter will probably find this
more helpful'.

In making connections to their own experience, group members will offer stories
of their own, as well as opinions and beliefs. This provides the researcher with
not only the story of the 'difficult situation' offered by the presenter, but also
additional data in story form from the other group members. The process is invariably
useful and interesting for the group members, with a range of insights and new
perspectives being gained from others' experience. The most commonly expressed
benefit is the experience of sitting outside of the group, after presenting. This is
often difficult – the desire to correct misunderstandings is great – but it is typically
enlightening to realise that there are other ways to make sense of the situation being
faced.

WORKING WITH THE DATA

Interpreting and analysing data in storied form can be challenging. For example,
while we are seeking stories that somehow represent the reality of the storyteller's
experience, this is clearly not 'reality' as it is understood in common usage – the story
is not 'factual information'. It is a construction, based on a memory of a recent or
distant experience. In Chapter 1 we noted the possibility that organisational members
may rely on self-presentation routines that are based in their competence and expertise
(Marcic, 2002). Even where it is based on a 'real experience', we must ask questions
about how it is constructed. Even if our research participants 'tell it as it is', we
must take into account the fact that they are constrained in the telling by the words
and language that are available – the constructed story may use the building blocks
of experience, but these are shaped with the tools of discourse that are available to
the storyteller. They will also have their own perspective and bias, which will have

constrained and influenced their experiences as much as they affect the telling of the story.

In addition, we are faced with a series of problems or challenges when we work with stories. For example, what was our purpose in telling you the story right at the beginning of the chapter? Was it to communicate 'a reality'? Or was it to engage, even seduce, you – to make you suspend your critical faculties and believe us just because we can tell a good story? Or was it narcissistic – just a bit of showing off? These are valid and important questions that you might bear in mind whenever you approach the analysis of the stories that you have gathered. The reason for this is that good stories are effective at doing all of these things.

In a similar vein, Gabriel brings our attention to the role of 'poetic licence', suggesting that storytelling enables the organisational member to express views that may be difficult or dangerous to voice directly. He suggests that such stories, being emotionally and symbolically charged narratives, do not merely represent information or facts about 'events'. Stories enrich and enhance facts, often compromising accuracy, and containing inconsistencies, illogicalities and ambiguities. Ultimately, Gabriel argues, the truth of a story lies not in its accuracy but in its meaning (Gabriel, 1999, p. 271)

All of these questions challenge the extent to which stories are providing us with an accurate and reliable source of data about organisational experience. This serves as a caution to the researcher to retain a healthy degree of suspicion concerning the extent to which the storyteller may change the story in the moment, for dramatic purposes. The telling of stories will always have this dimension, because of the nature of the medium and the process of social interaction. This becomes a matter of judgement for the researcher, but this judgement does not need to be made in a vacuum – there are certain principles that may be applied.

We can judge stories by evaluating narrative probability and narrative fidelity. *Narrative probability* is the coherence of the story: the extent to which it is free of contradictions, both internally and when compared to other stories, and is in keeping with the known characteristics of the individuals involved. *Narrative fidelity* concerns how well the story corresponds with experience, presenting good reasons for what happens, based on history, culture and biography, and so reflects the truth (Weick and Browning, 1986).

In learning to analyse the transcripts of stories, the organisational researcher needs to develop a capacity to make appropriate judgements in these matters. This is assisted by wider reading, as suggested in the discussion above of underlying theory. Nothing will tell us the 'best way' to analyse the stories we gather – as we suggested in Chapter 2, we must learn the art of the *bricoleur*, to play around with data. There are a vast array of ideas in some of the seminal texts on the analysis of qualitative data, for example Silverman (2001). In this way we practice analysis with a thoughtful awareness of the medium with which we work, gaining ideas from others about interesting approaches that might yield appropriate insights. The following two case studies present examples of this.

Case study 1: analysing the structure of stories

The first case study of working with data in storied form analyses the structure of a single story derived from an interview on 'what leaders do'. This is an example of using a framework from the literature to develop insights. This initial analysis began as a bit of 'playing around', but came to form the basis for the analysis of a series of interviews for similar ideas and themes.

Labov (1972) provides us with a framework for analysing the structure of stories. Labov suggests that there are five elements in a complete story: abstract, orientation, complication, evaluation and result. The following story, taken from the beginning of an interview with a very successful entrepreneur, was subjected to an initial analysis using this framework. This story is presented exactly as it was spoken and then recorded in the transcript. It just so happened that this matched Labov's framework precisely. It should be noted that this is not always the case. This is the story, broken into its component parts:

Abstract: I don't really like the concept of leadership.

Orientation: In fact, when I created the course at [the university], although it's called LIES [Leadership, Innovation and Enterprise], it was really about innovation and enterprise, we just threw in leadership to make it respectable.

Complication: Why I don't like it is if you know where you are going people are just likely to follow.

Evaluation: What matters is the enthusiasm needed to carry them along, and, if you are employing people, the power that goes with it: the guy that pays the wages is a great leader! You can confuse the giving of rewards with leadership.

Result: I think much more about people than I do about leadership. If you promised me a million pounds to name the people who work for our suppliers or our customers, I doubt that I could. But I can name the directors, the managers, the graduates and so on who work for us. Without going over the top, they need to know you care, that you recognise they have needs, that you are concerned.

The *abstract* introduces us to the theme of the narrative – and, as it turns out, to the key theme of the whole interview. With the *orientation*, he lays out the basic setting for this short narrative – the creation of the course and its name. The *complication* is signalled by the phrase 'Why I don't like it is …' In this case, the complication turns on its head the dominant image of the leader as 'prime mover'. The *evaluation* too

Continued

has a linguistic 'marker' in the phrase, 'What matters is ...' He tells us that you simply do not need this monolithic 'thing' – 'leadership' – because quite ordinary things are enough; here he specifically names relationships with others and organisational power. The *result* is not an extended discussion. In picking up some of the themes of the narrative, he simply tells us: as a result, this is what I do.

Our purpose was to identify 'rounded and full' (rather than 'partial and incomplete') stories in the text of an interview that lasted 90 minutes. The unexpected consequence, however, was that in slowing down and reflecting carefully upon the structure of the story we noticed some very unusual features in the arguments being made. In particular, we noticed the deconstruction of the notion of leadership by a leader who was being interviewed about 'what leaders do'. This then formed the basis of a content analysis of the rest of the interview, and indeed of other interviews in the series (French and Simpson, 2006).

Case study 2: playing around with themes or theories

The second illustration of working with data in storied form is the analysis of a section of the transcript from a group research project on 'difficult situations'. It demonstrates how, *once one discovers a theme or theoretical notion*, it is possible to *play around* with stories and interpretations to develop an argument. The theme, in this case, is that of paradox (Stacey, 2003).

This concerns a story told by Trevor, a parish curate who had a hostile working relationship with the Liaison Officer for those in the community with disabilities. Previously a social worker specialising in working with the disabled, Trevor had been asked by the Archdeacon to 'manage' this Officer, whose competency to perform the role was in doubt. The Liaison Officer was herself disabled and had recently been off work for a number of months following a family bereavement.

Trevor had agreed to take on this additional responsibility. Perhaps expecting gratitude at his willingness to volunteer, he was angered by the hostility and criticism that was directed at him by the Liaison Officer. The situation seemed impossible. During the discussion, one member of the research group, identified the need to work with a paradox:

The Liaison Officer is in that job whether Trevor thinks she's right or not, and she's got the support and authority that comes from the

Bishop and the Archdeacon, and she's been there for two years or so. It's very difficult. I've not had a lot to do with the disabled, but it is very difficult for able-bodied people to understand where they are coming from. The fact that she hasn't got high self-esteem and in some ways does not seem terribly competent may actually be a huge gift to the disabled community, because that's actually where they are coming from.

The paradox has two elements. Firstly, that Trevor had taken on responsibility to manage a situation, but did not have the authority to manage it in the way that appeared to him necessary (the replacement of the Officer). The challenge of responsibility without authority is a common issue that requires the leader to engage with a paradox: what is known to be possible is not possible because it is not allowed. Secondly, certain aspects of the incompetence of the Officer might be central to the Officer's competence to perform the role.

At the subsequent meeting of the research group, Trevor reported that, in the event, he had done nothing – but waited for something to happen. That something was a conciliatory move on the part of the Officer, saying that 'she realised that they needed to meet up'. Trevor's reaction was that this move could be used 'as a strength rather than a weakness':

> We talked a lot last time about the weaknesses of this person. The strength, for her and for me, is that she has not just flounced off and given her notice in, which would be detrimental at this time to the diocese. The fact that she is wanting things to work is quite encouraging.

Engaging with paradox requires a preparedness to meet on both sides. Waiting and doing nothing allowed the Liaison Officer to take the initiative. The positive outcome of this reminded Trevor of his social work training:

> Often you could see a situation in a private home where they clearly needed to move on to a residential nursing home or a mental health hospital, but they weren't ready to do that. I won't say it was *always* easy, but *on the whole* it was easy to walk back to Social Services and just write on the file, 'Waiting for this person to fall' … [Eventually] you would get a phone call either from them or from a relative to say, 'Actually I need to go'. If I had gone in and said you need to do this, that and the other it probably would have failed. Sometimes that can take 18 months, but it happened eventually.

Continued

> As well as re-learning an old lesson, Trevor noted the emergence of some self-knowledge:
>
> > The thing that has struck me since ... listening to what everybody was saying, is that I don't suffer fools gladly. I'm more conscious of that now than I was and it's not how I work with a fool – I don't mean that – but how I work with somebody who doesn't come up to the same expectations that I have ...
>
> These expectations of others, this knowledge of how competent the Officer should be, made it difficult for Trevor to work with the paradoxes of leading without authority and the potential competence of incompetence. However, the lack of a possible resolution, and the research process itself, compelled him to persist with this experience of not knowing.

CONCLUSION

Stories are one of the most common ways that people communicate and work with their experience. While stories are often told because they are interesting and engaging, they do much more than this. They are an essential component in the sense-making process – they can be used in problem-solving, socialisation, learning and other important aspects of organisational life. This means that stories can be an enormously rich and plentiful source of data for the organisational researcher. As a medium for research, stories are relatively easy to work with, with well-formed and coherent texts providing reasons and interpretations that can be worked with in the development of your research writing.

There is a great deal of research that has already been done in the area. This is helpful, but it does mean that there are many ways in which it is possible to use stories in research. It is important to be clear how you are going to use them in your research. In the Further Reading section we suggest an article by Mary Boyce that provides an excellent critical review of the literature up to the mid-1990s. This is particularly useful for locating and positioning yourself as a researcher, and contains some excellent examples of the ways that stories have been used in research and some challenges to the application of story work to organisations. This will be valuable in helping the researcher to clarify the way in which she or he wants to work with stories and the particular perspectives that are going to be adopted.

NOTES

1. This interview was part of a research project carried out by the author with Professor Charles Harvey and Dr. Robert French.

DISCUSSION QUESTIONS

1. What are the important differences between stories that are told and retold within an organisation, and those that are told to you, the research interviewer, perhaps for the first time?
2. How would you determine whether the story being told was true or not? What are the implications for your research if you discover that the story was not factually true?
3. How would you prepare differently for a 'facts-as information' interview and a 'facts-as-experience' interview?
4. What problems might you encounter when working with a group to elicit stories? In your preparation for the first meeting, what could you do that might help to ameliorate these potential difficulties?
5. What are the main challenges involved in interpreting and analysing the data that emerge from stories?

FURTHER READING

This book is concerned with methods of research that give attention to the social construction of reality and the development of a critical understanding of these realities. The 1996 article by Mary Boyce adopts this perspective, and so provides a very helpful overview of core ideas and literature on organisational stories and storytelling. For a more extended example of the practice of researching stories in organisations, Yiannis Gabriel's book is excellent. Finally, the task of interpreting your data will require some attention: David Silverman's guidance will be invaluable.

Boyce, M.E. (1996) 'Organizational Story and Storytelling: A Critical Review', *Journal of Organizational Change Management*, Vol. 9, No. 5: 5–26

Gabriel, Y. (2000) *Storytelling in Organizations. Facts, Fictions and Fantasies,* Oxford: Oxford University Press

Silverman, D. (2001) *Interpreting Qualitative Data – Methods for Analysing Talk, Texts and Interaction*, London: Sage Publications

CHAPTER 6

POETRY

Louise Grisoni

OVERVIEW

- How this method has developed
- What is poetry?
- Underlying principles and theory
- Different ways of using poetry in organizational research
- Case studies
- How to analyse and interpret the data
- Conclusion
- Discussion questions
- Further reading

And when old words die out on the tongue, new
Melodies break forth from the heart; and where the
Old tracks are lost, new country is revealed with its wonders.

(Rabindranath Tagore, *Gitanjali*, 1912)

HOW THIS METHOD HAS DEVELOPED

Using poetry as a creative research method is possibly the least researched of all the methods discussed in this book, and an early question for the reader might be: what does poetry have to do with organizational research? In Chapter 1 we discussed the assumption that giving attention to the rich and multifaceted dimensions of human experience can enhance research into social systems. This Chapter locates debates about connections between poetry and research into organizations and organizational life. It offers practical ways in which the researcher can work with different forms of poetry in order to access deeper insight into the emotional texture of social interactions.

Louise's favourite poem

The following poem by Robert Frost is a particular favourite of mine. I remember reading it many years ago as part of a leaving speech when I made a decision to change career. The decision to make this change felt brave, as I was on a successful career trajectory in my organization and I wasn't at all sure whether I was making the 'right' choice. At the same time, using poetry as part of a speech to colleagues, where I wanted to thank them for their support but also to recognize that I would be leaving them behind, felt risky – a bit self-indulgent perhaps, and I was concerned that the meaning in the poem would not be easily conveyed to others in a first reading. Since then I have returned to this poem several times, especially when I have been making difficult life choices and have wanted to trust my intuition and go with my tendency to take the path 'less travelled by'.

THE ROAD NOT TAKEN

Two roads diverged in a yellow wood,
And sorry I could not travel both
And be one traveller, long I stood
And looked down one as far as I could
To where it bent in the undergrowth;

Then took the other, as just as fair,
And having perhaps the better claim,
Because it was grassy and wanted wear;
Though as for that, the passing there
Had worn them really about the same,
And both that morning equally lay
In leaves no step had trodden black.
Oh, I kept the first for another day!
Yet knowing how way leads on to way,
I doubted if I should ever come back.

I shall be telling this with a sigh
Somewhere ages and ages hence:
Two roads diverged in a wood, and I –

Continued

> I took the one less travelled by,
> And that has made all the difference.
>
> (Robert Frost, 1973, *Selected Poems*)

Whyte (1994) provides a useful base from which to begin our exploration of poetry and research. In his exposition to turn to poetry, he speaks of a need to:

> bring together the supposedly strategic world of business with the great inheritance of the literary imagination, particularly through that difficult art poetry, and particularly through the fierce, unremitting wish for the dangerous truth that is poetry's special gift.
>
> (Whyte, 1994, p. xv)

Whyte has been invited by organizations to bring poetry to bear on certain aspects of change and creativity in the workplace. In working with many different companies, he has tried to illuminate specific steps along the path of change, and the forces that work for and against an individual who asks for more commitment and passion in their work. His approach is to use poetry in his consultancy practice:

> Rather than talk about change, I use hundreds of memorized poems to bring to life the experience of change itself.
>
> (Whyte, 1994, p. 9)

Whyte draws a parallel between writing poetry and poetry's place in the world, with the individual's work effort and its general benefit within and outside the organization. There is both an individual and a collective dimension in poetry: the individual poet writes alone, but, once shared, the poem belongs to everyone. The individual worker completes his or her tasks for some degree of personal satisfaction, but also for the organization's benefit. He speaks of how we are in a time when idealism is out of fashion, where there is an absence of compassion and a failing of imagination, and how new images can be found in poetry. He argues that poetry as verse or prose tends to be distinguished by its ability to move us deeply:

> No language matches good poetry in its precision about the human drama.
>
> (Whyte, 1994, p.18)

Whyte does not offer easy answers on the way home-life and work-life; career and creativity; soul and seniority, can be bought together. Windle (2006) also draws attention to the tension between corporate life and what he terms the 'fuller life', which includes:

> basic human yearnings – emotional needs and wider family, social and intellectual aspirations and relationships.
>
> (Windle, 2006, p. 457)

These, he argues, have in the past largely been excluded from, and thought irrelevant to, the corporate model of business. As has been discussed in Chapter 1, there has been a shift to include the 'fuller life', which is increasingly being addressed in organization studies literature, and Wheatley (2002) in particular incorporates poetry into her writing on how to generate conversations about experiences in organizations. As Windle says:

> From the unease of many individuals involved in business, the agenda widened to embrace the deeper needs of corporations themselves and their increasing influence on society. It was not an accident that the language of poetry was eventually invoked to help the change.
>
> (Windle, 2006, p. 457)

Whyte promotes poetry as a way of influencing conversations by accessing the emotions, desires and passions of organizational members. In this way, poetry cuts through the superficiality of many organizational encounters. Poetry can be seen as a way of connecting – through the medium of words and language – and helps us to see the world differently, which is important in relation to researching organizations. Kostera's (1997) work develops the contribution of poetry to research the relationship between feelings and organizing. She argues that poetry as an approach is well suited for expressing the ambivalence and volatility of the managerial experience. As such, poetry's strength as a research method is that it does not 'flatten out' the domains of organizing or 'translate them into rationality' (Kostera, 1997, p. 343). Kostera proposes that poetry can be used to understand more about organizational realities. Her aim in using poetry was to learn about the subversive and subjective experience of talking about management topics. She argues that poetry is particularly powerful, in that it does not avoid passion and it is disruptive because it is inconclusive.

The conclusion to be drawn so far is that organizational life is complex and multilayered, as it involves acknowledgement of emotions and relationships. Choosing to work with poetry in the research process to explore these issues is a powerful medium, as it can capture the richness of language and harnesses reflective processes that encourage expression of the complexity of organizational experience.

WHAT IS POETRY?

Poetry is probably one of the oldest ways of representing written 'knowledge', whether that knowledge was of the history of a people or of the playtime of the Gods. The Icelandic sagas, the poetry of Homer and of Beowulf, have all played their part in the definition of Western culture. Definitions of poetry are contentious and difficult. Samuel Johnson famously said, 'Why, Sir, it is much easier to say what it is not'. Some definitions offered below can help understanding.

Some definitions of poetry

'... a piece of writing in which the expression of feelings and ideas is given intensity by particular attention to diction (sometimes including rhyme), rhythm and imagery.'
'... a literary work in which the expression of feelings and ideas is given intensity by the use of distinctive style and rhythm'
'... a quality of beauty and intensity of emotion regarded as characteristic of poems.'

(from the *Oxford Dictionary of English*, Second edition, 2003)

Poets today commonly adopt a mix of several distinct viewpoints. For example, traditionalists would argue that a poem is an expression of a vision that is rendered in a form that is intelligible and pleasurable to others and so is likely to arouse kindred emotions. Modernists would say a poem is an autonomous object that may or may not represent the real world but is created in language made distinctive by its complex web of references. Postmodernists would view poems as collages of current idioms that are intriguing but self-contained – they employ, challenge and/or mock preconceptions, but refer to nothing beyond themselves. For all but postmodernists, poetry is an art form, and must therefore do what all art does – represent something of the world; express or evoke emotion; please us by its form; and stand on its own as something autonomous and self-defining.

A poem is unique to its author or authors; it is created in the common currency of its period, which will be reflected in the style, preoccupations, and shared beliefs held. There is an important point here about diversity, as all cultures seem to have their own poetry. Kostera (1997) says poetry is:

> not only an 'open text', but also an 'exploding text', a dangerous mode of expression, shattering space and embracing the reader with an invitation to reach out into the blank fields beyond 'information', outside the relatively safe territories of the orderly textual experience.

(Kostera, 1997, p. 346)

Poems are not created by recipe; shape and content interact in the final product and throughout the creation process, so that the poems will be continually asking what you are writing and why. The answers that you give yourself will develop, eventually to include experiences more viscerally part of you, since poems are not a painless juggling with words.

We are left with a question about whether poetry is good or bad and whether or not this matters when poetry is being used as a research method. To a certain extent, the answer will be subjective. Whyte suggests that a bad poem belongs exclusively to the writer and it could make a useful journal entry. Really good poetry has the capacity to engage all who read it. As he says, 'the work itself is compelling, as if someone has suddenly said something out loud in a crowded room that must be listened to, answered, or argued about for years to come' (Whyte, 1994, p.99). This thought may be off-putting to the novice researcher using creative methods and to those who are not poets but who wish to work with poetic forms in the creation of new knowledge about organizational experiences. The stance taken in this Chapter (and indeed the whole book) is an open one that encourages experimentation and playfulness with approaches to research methods. We would argue that it is important to pay as much attention to the relational processes involved in working with poetry as the final poetic product. Working in new creative ways may have the effect of disturbing established patterns of describing, explaining and analysing data, and as a result it may allow the opportunity for new understandings to emerge.

Key terms: characteristics of poetry

- *Theme* – The central meaning of the poem. Poets write to try to make sense of life and to convey their thoughts about nature, birth, love, death, families, growing up, and so on. Poets also create pictures of, and make comments on, social concerns like poverty, the environment, and technology. They tell stories and put abstract feelings into words.
- *Images* – The 'pictures' in the mind that the poet creates through language. Poets are astute observers; they see ordinary people, events, and objects in a fresh and original way. Poets are sensitive to the sights, sounds, smells, and textures of things around them. They see priceless moments and details, and they 'show' them to the reader through carefully crafted words.
- *Diction* – The selection of specific words. Poets choose words carefully and arrange them in the best order: they make every word count. Poets use rhyme and rhythm; alliteration and assonance; similes and metaphors and other poetic techniques to capture the essence of what they mean.

Continued

- *Poetic form* – The arrangement of words, lines, verses, rhymes and other features. There are different kinds of poems, each governed by its own set of rules for composition.
- *Haiku* – A Japanese poem of 17 syllables in three lines of five, seven and five, traditionally evoking images of the natural world.

UNDERLYING PRINCIPLES AND THEORY

When using poetry as a research method, it is helpful to have an appreciation of aesthetics, which is the study of forms and appearances (Strati, 1999; Taylor, 2002). As Linstead (2006) argues:

> When attempting to gain some insight into another group's culture, this sort of experience is exactly what questionnaires cannot provide and what the use of aesthetics – art, music, poetry, theatre and dance – provides brilliantly.
>
> (Linstead, 2006, p. 475)

Poetry provides representations of what people believe is happening to them, and is a vehicle for capturing these experiences, which can then be made available for interpretation (Grisoni and Kirk, 2006). Csikszentmihalyi and Robinson (1990) argue that aesthetic experiences are more important than supposedly objective experience. Adoption of a relational, dialogic stance in studying meaning in everyday practice, based on social constructions of reality, requires an interpretive method, which in relation to poetry is called 'social poetics' (Essex and Mainemelis, 2002). Poetics is concerned with the systematic study of texts as cultural artefacts, which focuses interest on the text construction; the authority or the text; and the production of meaning in discourse, as well as the representation and successful communication of experience. Connections may be between aspects of surrounding circumstances; between ourselves and others; and between action and sense (Geertz, 1983). As meaning is created by each person in interaction with others or the text, there is also a need to consider the 'role of the other' (Bakhtin, 1986), and research becomes an ongoing process of reconstructing and reinterpreting meaning. Social poetics is an example of a rhetorical practice because it offers a way of relationally engaging with others. Poetry provides information not only about situations but also reflects ways of relating to our surroundings and the circumstances of our lives (Cunliffe, 2002; Shotter and Cunliffe, 2002).

Saunders (2003), in her exploration of the relationship between poetry and research, summarizes her reflections as follows:

> poetry is a way of not having to conclude that there were no conclusions; the form as well as the intent is agnostic. It allowed us to be reticent ...

– to try to respect the integrity of the unknowable without being impelled
to remain wordless.

(Saunders 2003, p. 185)

Using poetry as a research method contributes to methodological debates within
qualitative research about the use of alternative methods of data representation (Ellis
and Flaherty, 1992; Brearley, 2000; Richardson, 2002). Brearley (2000) explores her
engagement with data representation in verse:

> So I began playing with the creative voices of
> Poetry, song and multi-media
> The creative forms had enough ambiguity to live
>   beyond the specific
> Enough substance to invite engagement

The use of poetry advocated in this Chapter is consistent with approaches to action
research where there is an emphasis on the integration of action and reflection, so that
the knowledge developed in the inquiry process is directly relevant to the issues being
studied. The democratic nature of the research process is important. Contemporary
forms of action research place great importance on collaboration between all those
involved in the inquiry project, aiming to help the individual practitioner develop
skills of reflective practice and organization and community members develop a
culture of open inquiry as part of their work-life, as well as to develop learning
organizations or communities of inquiry (Reason, 2001).

The integration of theory and experience is made possible through poetry,
as it represents understandings at the level of individual and group experience.
Höpfl (1995, p. 176) speaks of poetry as 'the expression of lived experience'. In
Richardson's study of the 'Poetic representation of interviews', she recognizes that
poetic representation is not the only or even the best way to represent all social
research knowledge. However, she does claim that for some kinds of knowledge
poetic representation may be preferable to prose; that it is a viable method for
seeing beyond social scientific conventions; and that it should be of interest to
those concerned with epistemological issues (Richardson, 2002, p. 877). There is
a strong argument for regarding poetry as a valid mode of communicating what
we know. Saunders (2006) proposes that poetry has a special and distinct contribution
to make, as it aims to:

- Present rather than argue;
- Offer insights rather than build theory;
- Add to a sense of the world's variety rather than negotiate and refine a consensus;
- Play (with ideas) rather than work towards a closure;
- 'Make new' rather than seek to replicate or systematically build on what has
  gone before;
- Proceed by association and image, rather than evidence and logical consequence;

- Engage, surprise, attract, shock, delight, connect the unconnected, stir the memory and fertilize the unconscious;
- Communicate something ultimately unsayable.

DIFFERENT WAYS OF USING POETRY IN ORGANIZATIONAL RESEARCH

Working with poetry as a management or organizational research method can involve different possibilities, including the creation of new works as well as working with recollections of existing works by established poets. Poetry can be used autobiographically for individual reflections on experiences – such as in the case at the beginning of this Chapter where my chosen poem provided insights into my decision-making preferences – and explorations of understandings. It can be used collectively, creating the potential for shared insights and understandings, resulting in the emergence of new forms of narrative. The argument presented here is that the world of business needs to work with poetry in order to gain insight into the complexity of relationships that form part of organizational life. Barry and Elmes (1997) take a narrative approach to their study of strategy, providing an interpretive lens which emphasizes multiple interlinked realities, a focus that is well positioned for capturing the diversity and complexity present in strategic discourse. Sense-making occurs through story-telling, and poetry augments this approach. In the first two case studies that follow, 'polyphonic' poems are created with dialogic authorship where 'different logics not only co-exist, but inform and shape one another' (Barry and Elmes, 1997, p. 444).

There are different categories of poetry, e.g. lyric, narrative, and dramatic. Within those three general categories, there are a number of different types, such as haiku, ode, epic, ballad and monologue. When working with groups creating poetry to capture aspects of organizational life or experience, it may be useful to create a focus by using a particular form of poetry. The sonnet form could be used – i.e. a strict 14-line poem with a set rhyming structure. Alternatively, other metrical forms, such as rap, could be used creatively. This increasingly familiar way of expressing emotion through song and performance could be a powerful format for research participants to explore the expression of diverse themes and ideas about organizations. There are many other examples: football chants, shape poems (where the words on the page create a graphical shape or representation), limericks, ballads or riddles.

Three different ways and examples of using poetry as a creative research method will be explored:

- People on an inquiry workshop writing poetry, for example a haiku – uncovering some unexpressed aspects of the organizational system. From this example, poetry is demonstrated as possessing the potential to access the essence of what might be happening in organizations (case study 1).

- Bringing a group of participants together to create collective, collaborative poems that help to develop new understandings of a research question, in order to draw out the themes and individual interpretations contained in the poems (case study 2).
- As a reflective, analytical tool to access inner thoughts and feelings. In this way poetry is used for personal reflection to deal with complexity and an analysis of previously unprocessed data (case study 3). This may involve drawing on a number of lines from poems that hold meaning for people, in order to gain insight into organizational experience. The poetry can be the individual's own words or someone else's (extant poetry) that resonate or connect. Poetry in this way can illuminate what the issues are in a focused way.

Case study 1: inquiring into organizational experiences

A group of 18 middle and senior public service managers spent time working together to create poetry from their current organizational experiences. The inquiry performed the function of exploring the organizational *zeitgeist* for this group of managers. The managers were asked to identify a recent incident which had affected them in some way, and which they were still thinking about. Each manager narrated this incident to a colleague, who noted down key words from the story. The pairs worked together to form the key words into a poem, using the haiku poetic form as a guide. The poems were read out and posted around the room, and the group was invited to draw out key themes and issues which appeared to be represented in the poems and which were felt to be significant. The group noticed metaphors, negative emotions and gender references in the poems, and spoke about the difficult time that many were experiencing in their organizations. The value of creating haiku poems from the stories was that the emotions and issues expressed were distilled in an intense and powerful way, enabling many to realize, look at and speak about their experiences in new ways that would not have been accessed through their usual forms of communicating together. This work had a cathartic effect on the group, and energy levels during the exercise were high, lifting spirits. It was reported later that doing this work was the first time that the group had laughed together.

Here are some examples of the poems created by the group:

> Positive and new
> She puts me in a corner
> She pisses me off.

Continued

Angry workshop, shock
Blown apart, back and forth farce
Fiasco, men usurp.

Ten million pounds down
Search parties – look in your drawers
So ~~ridiculous~~[1] hilarious!

Target high and lows
Expectations hit and miss
What to do? Worried.

An important learning point in this case is saying things through poetry that might not be communicated as effectively in any other way. The language is stripped down to its essence, and the key concept that emerges encapsulates a particular aspect of the experience. The process is essentially one of editing. Wherever possible, the original words are kept, and the words that seem to clutter rather than illuminate the core idea are discarded.

Case study 2: inquiring into a specific research issue using collaborative poetry

In this case a group of eight managers met to inquire into emotions at work. Once the question was agreed, the process took the form of each person writing down on a piece of paper a line or two that seemed to say something about their response to the research question. The paper was folded over (similar to the party game of 'Consequences'), and a key word chosen by the author as being significant in relation to the now-hidden contribution was written on the front of the paper. The paper was then passed to the next person, and the process was continued by the new author writing a couple of lines inspired by the key word and his or her developing thoughts and feelings in relation to the research question. This continued until everyone had written on each sheet. Eight poems were generated. Here are two examples:

Scrabbling over the cubicle walls	WALLS
The rigid barriers in my mind	BARRIERS
It feels like we're at the boundary, at the edge of something	BOUNDARY
Suppose I slipped off the edge?	EDGE
Push the learning to the edge of our creative capacities	CREATIVE
Grow, embroider, paint sculpt, write, create	

> Poetry created from words.
> My thoughts, your words … and feelings??? FEELINGS
> It's good for one's health to liberate those feelings
> That are rumbling around in you RUMBLINGS
> Rumblings as inner noise disturbs structure STRUCTURES
> Words – fail – me, all of them WORDS
> But what lies behind, beneath the words? BEHIND
>
> The managers knew each other and were curious about exploring this new territory for the first time. These contextual issues would have had an impact on what was written. The poems are collective creations; they allow everyone to have a voice, because the individual contributions are anonymous. The whole poem becomes coherent, and the relationship of the selected one-word prompts to the next line provides the stimulus for connecting links.
>
> Following the workshop, the poems were written up and distributed to all participants. We needed to get more of a sense of the meaning contained in these poems, and we invited participants to reflect on them and respond with a further narrative. The strength of the data lies in its ambiguity and potential for multiple interpretations and levels of engagement. Reactions to the poems are reported in the next section, which deals with the analysis and interpretation of data.

Having illustrated some ways in which poetry might be used as a research method (and before going on to our third case) we offer some ideas about some steps to take when embarking on this method, which is designed for a two- or three-hour process of creating, collecting and analysing data.

- The researcher should consider what it is that she or he wants to investigate. Is it something that is sensitive to the discovery of hidden thoughts and feelings? If the answer is 'yes', then poetry might be a suitable method to use.
- Decide if this is to be an individual activity or a group process.
- Creating a suitable atmosphere and boundary to the activity is important. Choose a comfortable place where participants in the process will feel relaxed enough to write about thoughts and feelings. Choose a time slot (say one hour) that will allow unhurried reflections to emerge.
- Provide paper and pens to all taking part.
- Introduce the research question and describe the method that you want to use, such as haiku (case study one) or consequences (case study two), or any other personal method of reflection drawing on poems from known authors or autobiographic reflections. Usually this part is done in relative silence, with little discussion about what to write between participants – it is essentially a reflective space.

- Reassure participants that there are no right answers and that no one will be judging the standard of poetry produced. The poems do not have to rhyme!
- Allow time (about half an hour) for participants to read out the poems to each other and to respond to what has been created. The researcher may want to record this part of the process, after ensuring that the participants agree to be recorded.
- The researcher may feel that participants need some more time to make sense of what has been created. Another hour spent discussing the poems may be appropriate at this point. On the other hand, it may feel appropriate to let participants have some space and reflect on the poems at leisure. Be sure to give clear guidelines and a time scale for responding to the poems.

When deciding to use poetry as a research method, it is important to think about special ethical and validity considerations. In doing so, we build on some of the points made about research ethics discussed in Chapter 2. Because of the element of surprise that is possible when research participants reveal possibly well-guarded thoughts, feelings and emotions, there is a need to be sensitive to the power of poetry to reveal data that, for a range of positive and defensive reasons, are usually kept hidden. Participants in a process that includes writing poetry will need to be made aware of the potential power of what is revealed and the emotional connection to the material that may be stirred up. Even then, it is not possible to anticipate all of the feelings that may be aroused, and the researcher will need to pay attention to providing a well-thought-through process for the activity and to ensure that the activity has clear boundaries which provide a 'safe enough' context.

A management researcher's story: Claire

I can remember when I first started using poetry as a research method. I shared poems that had emerged from my research data, and I was amazed by the reaction of the participants. Some were really angry, and everybody expressed some disbelief and confusion to start with. I wasn't prepared for the strength of emotion that the process created. The material consisted of poems created from interviews, without any padding. More considered reflections followed later. Clearly, some 'hot buttons' had been pressed. To begin with, the data presented back to them was in a form that was too sharp and raw for them to cope with.

Ethical practice requires that participants can withdraw from the process at any point, and that they are made aware that any poems generated will only be used with the permission of the authors. Occasionally, participants have preferred to keep their poems private and speak about the process of creating the poems and what they reveal as general learning points and insights. In most cases, the participants have been delighted and energized by their work and happy to share with each other and the researcher.

HOW TO ANALYSE AND INTERPRET THE DATA

This method is like the others in this book – open to multiple interpretations. Different meanings will emerge for every individual participating in the process. The validity of the data produced therefore rests on claims that poetry reveals possibly unknown thoughts and feelings that generate new understandings and new forms of knowing in relation to the research question. We cannot say what those findings will be, but we can seek to validate the method through its rigour – the consistent ability to reveal hitherto hidden depths to the focus of the research, and continuous and reflexive feedback loops within a collaborative relationship with research participants to check the emerging findings.

To help us to understand how we might analyse and interpret data in this approach, we begin by looking at examples of participants' comments generated from their reading of the poems as outlined in case study 2. It is important to accept that there is no single interpretation. Many possibilities emerge from the invitation to engage with poetry and make connections in ways that are meaningful for those involved. One participant developed a possible definition for working with the emotional experience of their management role.

An inquiry participant's reflections (see case study 2)

I read the first poem as a challenge to take a risk and acknowledge deep strong emotions, i.e. to do what you believe in – a sort of 'call to arms'. The second is more cautionary and hesitant. The third reads like the process of engagement, still with a scary warning in the middle. Poem four speaks of the balance between certainty and uncertainty – I think of the two sides of a coin. Is this a 'toss up' – an act of chance? Poem five seems like some kind of descent to chaos and nonsense/madness. Poem six seems to contain the depths of depression and difficulty. Poem seven seems to regain control, and the last poem presents emotion as the winning concept over words.

Is this then what working with emotion means for me as a manager? A battle which requires signing up on the side of emotion, hearing the warnings and still going ahead – struggling with balance of power between certainty and uncertainty and the dangers of falling into chaos – falling into the depths of depression before spotting when to reassert control and hopefully winning through in the end?

Another participant wrote of how surprised they were by the insights that reading the poems generated for them.

Another inquiry participant's reflections (see case study 2)

I looked at them today – and was surprised again! The final poems that we produced did make an impact on me. I genuinely had a feeling that we had indeed been enabled to create something that might say something! The key appeared to have been the 'Consequences' method. As I did it, I was aware of scrambling in my mind to find an idea I could start with and use – but then of having that idea, which was born of performance anxiety, broken up by the words left by the previous writer, in a way that disrupted my thinking and made me respond in the moment to a stimulus that was increasingly from the group. I was reminded of social dreaming, where the sense of any individual dream belonging to the individual who dreamt it – and saying something about that person – quickly (almost immediately) evaporates, and the dreams seem to become a reflection of the unconscious dynamics of the group/social setting. The image that comes to mind is of the poems as a kind of photograph – a 'snapshot' of the 'group mind' captured at that moment – but taken with a filter, which cuts some wavelengths out, in order to highlight others.

The reference to social dreaming (Lawrence, 1998) is interesting. Poetry has managed to tap the unconscious realm where psychoanalytical approaches are well placed to develop understandings about what is being expressed. The close links between psychoanalytical processes and poetry are explored by Canham and Satyamurti (2003). Case study 3 provides an example of working with these links. A manager has used reflective processes to capture her experience of a dream, and from that experience wrote an accompanying poem. Her poem contains analysis and interpretation of data presented in poetic form. The extension of these experiences into organizational life illustrates the complexity of emotions behind experiences with colleagues, and uncertainty behind management decisions and actions.

Case study 3: a contemplative researcher

The Dream (23/11/04)

In my dream I met up with a friend, Diana and her daughter, Lucy. I remember thinking that Lucy looked fairy-like with a delicate pale face and long glistening auburn hair. I knew that Diana had died recently, but I had definitely made an arrangement to meet up with her. As I approached her house I saw her husband sitting in an open-top sports car with another woman. They were uncomfortable when they saw me approaching and tried to make a rapid getaway. However, they were parked tightly between two other cars and needed me to lift their car up and help them manoeuvre. There was a bit of shunting, and I enjoyed having the power to 'help' them on their way.

We went to an Italian restaurant for a meal. Diana was well known there and several women came up to her and welcomed her as an old friend. She said that these people were like her new family and they had made her feel like she belonged with them. We ate our meal – a simple one of pizza, salad and a glass of wine. Suddenly there was a flurry of excitement and we all left the restaurant and climbed into a large black limousine. While we were in the taxi, one of the women presented me with the bill for the meal we had just eaten. In our hurry to leave the restaurant we had left without paying. The bill came to over $1000, which when converted came to something like £273 … and a bit.

I was astonished; we had only had pizza and one drink each. It was clear that in order to mix with these people I was expected to pay for all of them. Diana was encouraging me, as she felt the cost of joining this group was worthwhile. This was a significant turning point – I decided I would only pay for myself and I asked for an itemized bill. The atmosphere in the car turned threatening and nasty. I was worried that I would be trapped with this group, and the sense that extortion was their underlying motive made me decide to cut and run. As I ran away, my progress was slow and I knew I would be caught eventually. Would my stand in the taxi make the eventual outcome better or worse?

THE PRICE TO PAY

I meet with those who have died
In my dreams
Bringing their angel daughter
They show me what could be.

Separation makes those left behind uncomfortable
Agitated and nervous
Hiding, their lives continue –
They can't get away so smoothly.

We have power to lift and help them on their way.
Motives are not so generous –
Embarrassment.

Continued

> Friends make you feel welcome – part of
>   the family.
> Good food, company, a sense of belonging.
> There's always a price to pay –
> For joining
> Conversion reveals the true cost
> Is it worthwhile?
> Pay up or escape?
> Trapped
> Extortion
> Cut and run
> No trust
> Not enough progress
> Caught eventually
> Will it go better or worse?

Analysis of poetry can happen in a number of ways (Glesne, 1997). Analysis can take a narrative form, as shown in case study 2, or it can take the form of a poem, as shown above. Brearley (2000) discusses how a poem has the potential to be both a research finding and analysis. She argues that a different kind of reading is required when reading poetry with feeling – something goes in that can take root and become our own. When this happens, she says: 'We become part of conversation with the world, with the words on the page and with ourselves' (Brearley, 2000, p. 19). Poems can be created from transcripts of interviews and stories. Here is an example from Brearley's work with managers' experiences of transition in organizational life (Brearley, 2000, p. 21):

I AM FEELING THE DARK

I want to go back, but if I did return
There'd be no-one there
I just want everything to be the way it was
I am feeling the dark.

Discussions in groups following the reading of all the haiku in case study 1 instigated a range of thoughts and ideas about the current climate pervading public services organizations. As a result of the workshop, there was a realization that everyone had a story to tell of their experiences, and that the organization is made up of living, breathing, feeling individuals who all have a voice and a view. This felt like a new realization for many, brought into focus by the combination of using a form that requires brevity, which one participant described as 'cutting to the chase'. Standing back to review the poems also gave a different perspective on the public services – to many enabling the celebration of success. It was noticeable that a tremendous energy was generated in the group when creating the poems and, as one participant commented, 'playfulness is possible in a contained way'. The process was one of encouraging creativity and playfulness.

These comments seem to confirm that the conditions necessary for enabling new knowledge creation (Von Krogh *et al.*, 2000) had been met. Through a process of poetry creation, conversations involving shared local knowledge, understandings, and experiences, were facilitated and new relationships established. A deeper sense of new emotional knowledge and care emerged from the poems, highlighting how people treat each other in the face of difficult organizational challenges.

CONCLUSION

Poetry holds the potential to capture emotion and express the unsayable with passion, truth and intensity. The choice about whether or not to use poetry is concerned with whether the topic or issue to be researched requires a reflective space that taps into emotions and uncovers layers of thought and feelings. Poetry is able to explore the shadow side of experience as well as the light, and it juxtaposes the rational realm with the emotional and unconscious. Creative forms of research invite active engagement, where those who engage in the process become co-creators of meaning in a way that blurs distinctions between researcher and participant, writer and reader, method and analysis.

Configuring and reconfiguring words in different ways, in poetic forms, enables us to understand and feel the world differently. We have shown that using poetry as a research approach is a practical and accessible way of approaching the heart of people's experiences and feelings within social systems. In Chapter 4, it is argued that the researcher who wants to use art and drawings does not need to be an art therapist and participants do not need to be good artists, and similarly in this Chapter I have argued that the researcher does not need to be a poet, and neither do the research participants. It is just that, with their permission and engagement, participants are being invited to participate in a creative process that may very well give novel insights and perspectives into their worlds.

As with all the creative methods covered in this book, the specific procedures involved in using this method may be adapted to suit particular research questions, and they may be responsive to participants' ideas. Be creative! The best thing is that, when something emerges that was not anticipated, something new has been created in terms of method and in terms of the discovery of new knowledge.

NOTES

1. We have retained the crossing out from the original.

DISCUSSION QUESTIONS

1. Can you think of rap or hip-hop as a poetic form, a means of self-expression facilitated by a highly rhythmic and 'funky' beat? Conduct a workshop as a form of karaoke, as a 'fun' event. Set up a sound system that can play appropriate backing tracks. Ask participants to rap (individually or in pairs) in addressing a particular research topic.
2. What is your favourite poem? Similarly, ask participants to choose their favourite poem, one that speaks powerfully to them – about life in general or in relation to the research topic, for example personal or organizational change and transition. Ask participants to read their chosen poem, and outline its significance for them.
3. Alternatively, as the researcher, provide research participants with a range of published poems, and ask them to choose one that holds significance. Carry out similar processes to the one suggested above.

FURTHER READING

A special issue of *Management Decision* (James and Weir, 2006) has explored the relationships and connections between five key words – poetry, organization, emotions, management and enterprise – and this issue brings together a collection of writings that link the worlds of poetry to business and management. In addition, two authors in particular are credited with adding to our understanding about the place of poetry in understanding organizational life: David Whyte's (1994) *The Heart Aroused* and Ralph Windle's (1994) *The Poetry of Business Life*. Both set out an agenda for connecting poetry and management. Windle challenged an assumption that not many people in business feel an urge to write verse about their work, and his anthology was presented as an 'assertion and a challenge'. It has become 'part-prologue and part stimulant' to the increasing cross-over between poets and the wider business world. Windle is a poet who has published in the *Harvard Business Review* and the *Financial Times* under the pen name Bertie Ramsbottom, and an article by him is included in the special issue of *Management Decision* referred to (Windle, 2006). He is former Director and Divisional CEO of Nabisco, UK, and his edition contains poetry written by a range of business people, including managers at all levels, as well as technical and support staff in a range of different organizations. Whyte is also a published poet, and has an established consulting practice among the boardrooms of the *Fortune* 500. He argues for the need to rediscover through the medium of poetry the heart and soul in business practice. He hoped that his work would be read in two ways; firstly as a good story about the difficulties and dramas of preserving the soul at work, and secondly as a public document encouraging conversations which will help us to re-imagine ourselves more fully in the workplace.

James, J. and Weir, D. (2006) 'Special Issue on Poetry, Organization, Emotions, Management and Enterprise – POEME', *Management Decision*, Vol. 44, No. 4: 453–456

Whyte, D. (1994) *The Heart Aroused: Poetry and the Preservation of the Soul in Corporate America*, New York: Doubleday

Windle, R. (Ed.) (1994) *The Poetry of Business Life*, San Francisco, CA: Berrett-Koehler

ACKNOWLEDGEMENT

'The Road Not Taken' from *The Poetry of Robert Frost*, edited by Edward Connery Latham © 1969 by Henry Host and Company.

CHAPTER 7

MASKS AND THEATRE

Philip Kirk and Robert French

OVERVIEW

- **What this approach is and why use it**
- **History and origins of the ideas**
- **Underlying principles and theory**
- **Theatre of the mind**
- **Organizations as theatre**
- **Applying masks and theatre in organizational and management research**
- **Case studies**
- **Analysis and interpretation of data**
- **Conclusion**
- **Discussion questions**
- **Further reading**

WHAT THIS APPROACH IS AND WHY USE IT

For many people, it is a common experience to sometimes feel as if we might be wearing a mask or acting a part. Perhaps in a group at work or in an unfamiliar social gathering, we can find ourselves behaving in ways that do not feel quite like our usual selves, and yet seem to be appropriate in the situation. We may have been conscious of trying to hide a feeling of being uncomfortable, or trying to project an image of some kind, such as being in control, cool, calm and collected, when underneath we were anything but! It is possible that we may not have thought of ourselves as wearing a mask at all. It is only looking back after the event that we may catch ourselves thinking: 'Was that really me doing that, saying that?' Or someone who knows us says: 'You were very different to how you normally are – I hardly recognized you'. It is at such points that we come to realize that we were acting or, as it were, wearing a mask, in order to be someone different or to put ourselves across differently.

This chapter describes the use of 'masks and theatre' as metaphors that offer a different angle on organizational inquiry. They provide a perspective that an organizational or management researcher can use to identify and make sense of the unfolding dramas of organizational life, whether these are ordinary, day-to-day events or more unusual and 'dramatic' ones. Potentially, such dramas come in many forms – as histories, comedies or tragedies, improvised or with set parts. Using masks and theatre as a method of inquiry can allow both researcher and research participants to gain access to their experiences and explore their actions, thoughts and feelings, in different and creative ways, with the possibility of new insights and understandings. The method can make it possible for people to engage in the inquiry in active, imaginative and intuitive ways, as they use the metaphors to describe events and seek explanations.

Two examples of mask and theatre in work contexts

The selection interview

An interview sometimes feels just like a play on the stage, with the actors in the drama having their separate parts. The interviewing panel plays its role and the interviewee does the same, and there are ritualized scripts and actions at different moments – set pieces almost: the opening greeting and handshake ['To play my part right, I must make sure my handshake is firm enough'], followed by the prompt 'Do sit down and make yourself comfortable'. [Return the smile at this point, and move a little in the chair to show that you are now fully relaxed.] At the end, there is another set piece: 'Do you have any questions for us?' – whether you have any or not, you know something is expected, so, having already learned your lines, you now hope that you won't 'dry up' … Suspense, dramatic tension, stage fright, props and costume: all of these play their part in the overall 'performance'.

Telephone inquiries

In this case, there is no need to *imagine* a scripted conversation, because these conversations often literally *are* scripted. The customer-service operators do actually learn their words. After the musical overture and the recorded voice that thanks you for waiting, appreciates your patience, tells you how important your custom is to them … finally you may be put through to an operator – only to find that their responses are as programmed as the recorded ones.

YOU ARE NOW
GOING ON STAGE

Figure 7.1   Staff Notice in a Department Store

The notice in Figure 7.1 was pinned on the wall by the management of a shop in Bristol. As it was placed 'behind the scenes' or 'in the wings', the words were visible to staff, but not to customers. And the staff were indeed always friendly and helpful – or so it seemed ... But were they just 'acting'?

Let us suppose that the organizational researcher's plan might be to focus on management, perhaps, or on organizational culture or customer relations – and she or he has the chance to do their fieldwork in this shop. The wording of the notice, especially the phrase 'on stage', is the first thing that strikes the researcher. She or he realizes at once that metaphors relating to acting or to the theatre may have a special significance in this particular organization, and hence for the research. An experience of this kind might suggest that this is a setting in which the research approach could be informed by, or even based on, the notions of masks and theatre.

How might the project take shape? What the researcher decides to do is to trace the way the metaphor is used in the company, and to assess its impact on the way that staff work. At one level, for instance, the language in general use in the organization might be observed, to see whether the metaphor appears in documents or in staff induction and training events. Then the analysis might move from language to action – from 'scripts' to 'performance' – by looking at how the shop(-as-theatre) is (stage-)managed. For example, data could be gathered by observing staff behaviour 'on' and 'off' stage; that is, the way that they talk about customers and products, and the way that they interact with each other 'backstage', compared with the way they 'perform' once they emerge from the wings to go 'on stage'. The researcher might take note of the arrangement of the shop generally, and the shop window in particular, in terms of layout and lighting, and see whether staff are required to – or choose to – wear clothes as a form of 'costume'.

Depending on the level, length and depth of the research, all the researcher might do would be to observe staff and customers for half an hour or so. On the other hand, he or she might be given gain access to written documents and to senior-management meetings, or may have an opportunity to interview staff, including managers at local, regional and/or national levels, and even customers.

Of course data collection is one thing; analysis is another. Here again, the metaphor of the theatre could have a creative application. The researcher could, for example, use data to generate theories about management or customer relations as 'illusion': theatre entertains, or conveys a message, precisely by creating an illusion, as do masks.

So what illusion was intended with the instruction: 'You are now going on stage'? One obvious hypothesis might simply be that the better the illusion created by sales staff the more money the shop will take: the better the performance, the more likely the sale. However, there might be others, such as the desire to outperform the competition. Alternatively, theories might be developed about power relations: to what extent did the 'director' take control in a rigid way, telling staff both what to say and how to say it, or did he or she just 'set the scene', make the 'plot' clear and give an idea of 'character', leaving the 'actors' to 'improvise' and to respond individually to their 'audience'?

A focus on the metaphor of theatre *as a research method* could help the researcher focus on both data collection and analysis, by holding the metaphor of theatre in mind: front of house; stage management and stage directions; scripts; learning and rehearsing one's part; losing the plot and having to be prompted; role and play-acting; props and scenery; audience reaction; box-office success ('takings'); farce; comedy; tragedy. ... It will be remembered that the metaphorical nature of the data that can be generated was discussed in Chapter 1 as one of the assumptions that underpin the effective use of creative methods in organizational and management research.

These ideas stem from a concrete example: the 'going on stage' notice in Figure 7.1. It was this phrase or text, produced by management, that drew attention to the staff–customer relationship as a performance. However, the metaphor itself opens up a rich seam, with potential applications in *any* organizational or social setting.

THE HISTORY, ORIGINS AND USES OF MASKS

The use of masks has evolved over thousands of years, from the story of Jacob and Esau in the Hebrew Scriptures to Homer's *Iliad*; to comic-book heroes like Batman and Green Lantern, or the mysterious powers of the mask in the film of the same name. Nunley *et al.* (1999) in their book, *Masks: Faces of Culture*, say that the origins of the word 'mask' are unclear, but that it probably came from the Arabic *maskhara* (*Mashara*), which meant 'to falsify' or 'transform'. In old Italian this became *maschera*, and it finally entered English as *mask*. In her book, *Masks in Modern Drama*, Susan Harris Smith (1984) says that the mask, because it conceals and shields the face, is as much a disguise as it is a protective covering:

> The mask is unique. ... it simultaneously hides and represents the face –
> the most vulnerable and revealing part of the body and the object of the
> most visual attention.
>
> (Harris Smith, 1984, pp. 183–184)

During the Renaissance, 'mask' came to mean disguise or pretence, whereas previously its primary social uses had been for a protective cover and, in the theatre, for character identification.

Another social function of the mask was that of transformation. In *The Other Face: The Mask in the Arts*, Walter Sorell (1973) says that belief in the mask's power to transform was well established in early society. Since early times, people have recognized that social life is a mix of many ingredients: truth and fiction; what is expressed and public and what is hidden and private; the physical and the spiritual. The boundaries between these are managed by social norms as well as individual choice. Sorrell says that in earlier societies the borders between the concrete and the symbolic were more blurred, less clearly demarcated; masks were one means whereby boundaries were crossed and transformation was made possible.

If masks can protect and disguise and transform, they can also reveal identity. They can enable us to divulge secret thoughts or hidden aspects of ourselves and our personalities that we ordinarily hide or feel unable to express. The power of anonymity gives us protection to behave in ways that we otherwise might not: to act aggressively, for example, or to break the rules. Thus, masks are a most ancient means of changing identity by assuming a new persona or of revealing identity by subverting our familiar defences (Nunley *et al.*, 1999, p. 15). That subverting was evident in the obsessive works of the Belgian expressionist painter James Ensor (1860–1949) – for example, see Figure 7.2 – in which it is not always clear whether the subjects in the

Figure 7.2   James Ensor, *Self-Portrait with Masks (1899)*. © DACS 2007

painting are wearing masks or not. In this example, however, Ensor's appears to be the only real face that is present in a sea of bizarreness. Of course, what is real and what is not is a vexed question. There are different views about whether wearing a mask reveals reality or hides it. According to Oscar Wilde in 1891, 'Man is least himself when he talks in his own person. Give him a mask and he will tell the truth.' The philosopher Jean-Jacques Rousseau, on the other hand, thought that when the mask falls, the person is revealed (Sorell, 1973, p. 13).

One evolution of the use of masks was in the world of theatrical performance. A theatrical mask was also known in ancient Greek theatre as a *'persona'* – something through which we speak: *per* meaning 'through', and *sona* 'sound'. Thus, 'personality' and 'mask' are directly linked: when we speak to each other, we do not so much talk directly one to one, as speak through the mask of role. However much we would like to think that it is just 'me' speaking, it is, in reality, 'me-in-the-role-of researcher', for example, or of brother, father, colleague, teacher, friend, or customer. Rather than speaking person-to-person, as we would like, often we speak *persona*-to-*persona* – mask to mask.

So whether we go back to ancient societies or simply look about us today, the idea of mask has an important place in the human psyche. We may wear masks for real in masquerades and carnivals, or we may just 'put on a face' – or even be 'two-faced' – in the different situations of our daily lives. And masks and theatre are closely linked. Because the wearing of masks has always been a social act, serving a social function, the 'drama' being played out in the wearing of the mask becomes 'theatre'. For masking to have meaning and relevance, it needs a theatre and an audience (Nunley *et al.*, 1999, p. 17). Susan Harris Smith suggests that people's irrational, imaginative and fanciful observations and feelings can be given temporary form and, consequently, a temporary reality by the wearing of a mask. In effect, she says, the mask turns the world into a temporary stage (Harris Smith, 1984, p. 3).

Given their impact on human experience over thousands of years, it is not surprising to find the vocabulary of masks and theatre richly represented in everyday language.

The metaphor of theatre and stage in everyday language

- role – getting into role; learning a part; learning a script (by heart)
- performance; improvisation; role-play
- acting the part; just play-acting
- acting-up (for example, as Head of Department)
- losing the plot
- setting the scene; going on stage

Continued

- a lecture 'theatre'
- the 'theatre' of war
- behind the scene; in the wings; backstage
- in the limelight; shining the 'spotlight' on an issue
- what a tragedy; it was a farce!
- scripts, speeches
- actor
- director, star, prima donna, extra, lead role, leading actor

Other parallels exist in terms of:

- 'props'– clothing ('costume')
- 'make-up'
- *actions*, rather than words
- 'scenery' (furniture, decoration, paintings)
- the timing of 'entrances' and 'exits'.

UNDERLYING PRINCIPLES AND THEORY

In this section, we address two ideas: the 'theatre of the mind', which concerns the inner world of the individual, and 'organizations as theatre', which concerns the person in his or her organizational setting.

The theatre of the mind

In *Theatres of the Mind*, psychoanalyst Joyce McDougall (1986) uses Shakespeare's words: 'All the world's a stage/ And all the men and women merely players', to introduce the image of theatre as a description of 'psychic reality'. She shows just how hard it is for us to escape our roles in an unfolding life drama whose plot is uncannily repetitive:

> Each of us harbors in our inner universe a number of 'characters,' parts of ourselves that frequently operate in complete contradiction to one another, causing conflict and mental pain to our conscious selves.
>
> McDougall, 1986, pp. 3–4

She goes on to point out that these inner characters constantly seek 'a stage on which to play out their tragedies and comedies'. The resultant 'plays' may be performed in the inner theatrical worlds of our own minds or bodies, but equally in the external world, 'sometimes using other people's minds and bodies, or even social institutions as their stage' (McDougall, 1986, p. 4). It is this link to organizational life – to 'social institutions' – that is the psychic foundation for the use of theatre and masks in research.

The complex co-existence of more-or-less complete, more-or-less mature identities within each of us has been described in a variety of other, similar images, such as a 'community' or 'parliament' of selves (Mead, 1934; Mair, 1977; Hobson, 1985). Each suggests a different 'flavour' or 'culture' to the relationship between the diverse 'selves' or part-selves we each carry within us: 'community' points at least to a *desire* for co-operation; 'parliament' has overtones of conflict, with the potential dominance of one 'side' or 'party' over others; and 'theatre' picks up on the ideas of some co-ordinating activity on the part of writer, director and manager, of us learning our scripts and roles, and of the existence of a 'lead' actor alongside various 'bit' parts.

The concept of a 'social self', as distinct from a merely private one – the self as a player of parts – was introduced by William James in *Principles of Psychology* in 1890 (James, 1957), and is further developed in a variety of theoretical fields, such as sociology, psychology and psychoanalysis. Sociologist Erving Goffman, in his book *Presentation of Self in Everyday Life* (1959), used the metaphor of theatre to show how people present themselves in their relations with others and in their interpretations of the responses that they receive. In this way, people create their social roles, allowing for organizing and co-ordination (Hatch *et al.*, 2005, p. 48). As Shirley Brice Heath (2000, pp. 9–10) says:

> A sense of self-identity and of the projected self never lies entirely 'within'
> but always in dialectic constructions of how one appears to others.

These are at once constructions that occur through the immediacy of current interactions, but are also based on assumptions drawn from prior experience as well as from deeply embedded prejudices and stereotypes. In this way, social life can be seen as a 'mutually contrived performance' (Hatch *et al.*, 2005, p. 48).

The self in relation to others is also seen in Berne's work on transactional analysis, *Games People Play* (1970). He suggests three 'ego states' that reside in any individual, those of 'Parent', 'Adult' and 'Child'. As individuals interact, these different ego states unconsciously shape the nature of those interactions. So interactions between two people may be 'Adult to Adult', or 'Parent to Child' and so on. By analysing the 'scripts' of these interactions between people, Berne says participants may become aware of how they are relating to each other, thus opening up the possibility for change.

Organizations as theatre

Many of the issues that relate theatre and organizational life can be brought into focus around the ubiquitous notion of 'role'. 'Role' originated in the theatre and was translated to the broader organizational context in the seventeenth century. Originally, it referred to the 'roll' of paper or parchment on which the words to be read by the actor were written. All the actor had to do was to read clearly the words written for him or her on their 'roll' as it unrolled in front of them. The scope for personal interpretation was severely limited. In rather the same way, roles in traditional or bureaucratic organizations tend to be prescribed or defined 'by the book'.

These historical roots in the theatre can lead to the idea of an organizational role being associated with not being real – with putting on a false face. The assumption is that to take on a role is to act out someone else's drama. Yet, for Briskin (1998), there is another way of looking at role. Finding and taking up one's role is for him tantamount to finding one's voice. It is through the role that authentic voice is able to find its expression and authority (Briskin, 1998, p. 195).

Today, however, the skills demanded of both the theatrical and organizational 'actor' are quite different; just 'reading from the script' is no longer enough. In an age of improvisation, the actor's role now tends to be much freer and, arguably, also more demanding, so that the most critical skill for the accomplished actor – theatrical or organizational – is the ability to *get into role*. This means understanding the overall context and tasks to which the role relates, including knowing one's audience and fellow actors (or clients and colleagues), and then testing that understanding by *creating the role in action*, not just reading from the 'roll'. Thus, role is a social concept. Organizational 'actors' take up their roles at work in relation to one another, and it is their ongoing interactions that produce the 'live theatre' of organizational life (see Mangham, 1986; Mangham and Overington, 1987).

In an organization or enterprise, 'role' provides a way of finding and making our contribution. Whether it is in a social club, in the family, at work, or indeed on the stage in a theatre, we speak of having a role. It provides the framework of meaning and purpose that shapes our identity and our actions in those settings: who and how we are, and what we do. According to Reed:

> To take a role implies being able to formulate or discover, however intuitively, a regulating principle inside oneself which enables one, as a person, to manage what one does in relation to the requirements of the situation one is in.
>
> (Reed, 2001, p. 2)

The relationship between theatre and organizations has increasingly been explored in recent years (see Boje *et al.*, 2003; Hatch, *et al.*, 2005). In drawing attention to this, in a special issue of the journal *Organization Studies*, Schreyögg and Höpfl point to the potential of using the notion of 'theatre' as a vehicle for organizational inquiry. For them, it broadens the scope of organizational analysis and provides fresh insights into organizational dynamics, both by looking at *organizations as theatres*, and by looking at *theatre in organizations* (Schreyögg and Höpfl, 2004, p. 691).

Organizations as theatre is a way of looking at real events and dramas that take place as people in the organization interact and go about their work. It provides an opportunity, through the lens of theatre, to see how individual and group performance is directed, how roles are enacted, how social control is exerted. Two examples illustrate how this can happen. A manager may be interested in exploring her or his own experiences of taking up a new role in the organization, and finds the use of *costume, mask, role, stage, script, performance* to be helpful 'tools' to reflect on his or her ongoing experiences, to make sense and to shape future action (see Torbert, 2001 for a commentary on first-person action-research methods). Another example may concern the experiences of two groups or two companies that have merged, or are in the process of merging. Again, the use of 'theatre' as a framework for analysis can provide an interesting way for participant researchers, who are involved in the experience, to replay and unpack that experience in creative and less-threatening ways, offering critical insights into such concepts as culture, identity, power relations, leadership, group norms, or operating assumptions (see Mienczakowski and Morgan, 2001, for an example of this, using ethnodrama as a research method).

Theatre in organizations is increasingly common at work, as employees role-play on management development programmes; take part in pantomimes at Christmas parties; or attend events (perhaps the annual conference) staged by top management to herald in a new mission or venture. An Anglican bishop, for example, recently embarked on a high-profile and well-received 'road show', where he toured different churches in the diocese, sharing his vision for the diocese in the coming decade. The use of theatre may be part of the enculturation process, where ritual enactments of past events are recounted to embed existing or long-held organizational values. On the other hand, they may be used as organizational interventions to destabilize and change – heralding a new way of acting and interacting.

Figure 7.3 sketches the two domains of the metaphor 'theatre': *organizations as theatre* represents an 'external' focus, while *theatre of the mind* represents an 'internal' focus. The process of '*masking*' is evident in both domains.

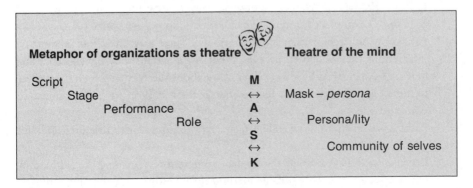

Figure 7.3   Two Domains of the Metaphor 'Theatre'

APPLYING MASKS AND THEATRE IN ORGANIZATIONAL
AND MANAGEMENT RESEARCH

So what kinds of research projects are possible using the metaphor of mask and theatre? The purpose of this section is to stimulate thought about possible options, by presenting a selection of possible ideas, rather than to provide an exhaustive list of ideas. The metaphors of mask and theatre could be used in a great variety of research situations of different scale and scope, some relatively short, others longer and more involved, some quite brief and straightforward, and others leading to more intense experiences. What they have in common, however, is that they offer the potential for looking differently at organizational events – a glimpse behind the scenes of organizational life, as it were.

So the researcher could use the metaphor of mask and/or theatre as an aid to *really looking* and *really listening*, in one of the following ways:

1. Observe an organizational event: a work meeting, a company's annual general meeting, a retirement presentation, a selection interview, an appraisal interview.
2. Observe a location: the reception area, the atrium, a working office, a shop.
3. Show a group a video of an episode of a programme such as '*The Office*', which is set in a workplace. Question: How is your office like/unlike this?
4. Make a brief audio-tape (say 30 minutes) of an office or other workplace, so that the group can hear the sounds of this office at work. The recording can then be analysed like a radio play.
5. Research into team dynamics: ask a 'team' to create three masks, representing *past, present, future*. They can then talk about the process. Or, once the masks have been prepared, ask the members to take any of the masks to say what they want to say in relation to how the team works. Alternatively, three participants could be asked to take a mask each and interact via the masks. At any point, other participants could tap one of the actors on the shoulder and take over as mask bearer.
6. Print off the day's email correspondence and analyse the 'scripts' to see what roles the person played in those email conversations.
7. Ask your research participant(s) to review their day: to think about the interactions they had with people. What masks could they have been using in each exchange? Why? What does it say about the way in which they relate to these people? Would they like to change their mask in any case, and if so to what and why?
8. Ask a work group to write and perform a pantomime with a title such as: 'This year in 10 minutes'.
9. Because masks have been used in so many different ways around the world, they might offer a particularly suitable method for investigating cultural differences. In some cultures, for example, the very worst thing that can happen is to

'lose face'. An ongoing inquiry into the impact of role in a multicultural setting might gain significantly in depth by asking the group to produce masks that represent key roles, such as manager or leader, supervisor or friend.

We would like to take three of these methods, and see how they may be used in practice. We present these in the form of case studies. The third case study is presented in greatest detail.

Case study 1: masks and learning in a culturally mixed student group

This is an account of some of the issues faced by a Chinese student, undertaking an MBA Dissertation, as she shaped her research project. Jenny is part of a class of 20 students who are from different countries: the UK, other European countries, Africa, the Indian subcontinent and the Far East. She wants to find out what impact the different cultural backgrounds of students had on the classroom experience for the students and the staff on the programme. Her aim was to use her research to develop the theory and practice of learning in a cross-cultural context.

Jenny plans to have an individual email conversation with all students and staff involved in the programme, asking them to describe their experience. She will also ask them to provide basic 'tick box' biographical data (such as age, gender, country of origin, extent of work experience). She is considering whether also to conduct group interviews with students and staff, where she will give feedback of her analysis of the 'email conversations' so that they can discuss the implications.

Jenny's use of the computer for data collection has the advantage that the data is already stored electronically on her own computer, opening up various ways to analyse the data. She could, for example, pick out key words or phrases from each response, that capture ideas or emotions. By comparing these across the responses, she can see if any patterns are emerging and, if so, whether these patterns tend to group by cultural background, age, gender, work experience, and so on. In addition, she could use the theoretical concepts from her reading of the literature on culture and learning, in order to categorize and interpret the data. For example, she could test the applicability to the data of Hofstede's (1991) national cultural classifications on learning: 'power–distance', 'masculinity–femininity', 'uncertainty avoidance', 'individual–collective'. She could then further analyse the data to pick out the extent to which student and staff learning-style preferences

Continued

(such as 'teacher-centred' or 'independent learning') related to the cultural dimensions listed above.

It will be seen from this account that, by following a procedure of this kind, Jenny could complete the research and analysis on her own, analysing the data, and giving herself the task of drawing out the implications for the theory and practice of learning in culturally mixed student groups. However, this 'first-level' analysis could then be subjected to a 'second-level' analysis, in which it was presented to the original research groups in order to work with their responses and develop implications.

In moving to a second level of analysis, Jenny need not use the metaphor of mask at all. She might simply ask the participants to describe their experience of being part of a culturally mixed student group; the impact this cultural mix has had on their individual learning; and its effect on the different nationality groups present. However, by using the metaphor of the mask, she might also gain a different level of insight, and open up conversation and dialogue about the subject more easily. She could, for example, add questions such as the following:

- Imagine the classroom as a theatre, with people there wearing different masks. What masks are being worn and by whom (including you)? Picture the scene in your mind and see if you can describe the drama of this mask-wearing. What effect is it having on learning?
- What mask best reflects your own national culture? What was its influence on your learning, if any?
- What masks reflect the other national cultures present in the class? How do you think this has affected learning?

If she wished to proceed to this second level of analysis, then it would clearly involve extra work: i.e. organizing and then facilitating group meetings and finding a way to record the data from the group discussions. This additional level of research could make the research richer, by building research-participant collaboration into the analysis and interpretation of the data and into thinking about future implications and applications.

There is, however, another side to this approach: it all adds volume and complexity to the research. As a result, the researcher will have to ask him or herself whether she or he has the time; the ability to get the groups to come together for the meetings; and the skills required to facilitate the meetings. In research, as in much else in life, we have to cut our suit according to our cloth. Finally, he or she would have to capture the data produced by the 'mask event' – via field notes and/or audio-tape or (ideally, perhaps) video recordings – and find an appropriate way to analyse this additional set of data.

Case study 2: observing a location

This is an example of a relatively straightforward, small-scale research exercise that could be undertaken by an organizational or management researcher. The research question is: 'What does the drama we observe tell us about an organization's culture'? *The method* is to go to the entrance of an organization and, for just half an hour, to observe the 'drama' of the comings and goings into and out of this organization. The issues that need to be addressed at the planning stage might include the following:

- Which organization? We will assume here that access has been negotiated and agreed. However, where is the entrance? The company may have a number of entrances. What is the cultural message in this alone? The issue would apply differently for any organization observed.
- How should we collect the data? And what would it look like? The architecture of the building is clearly one aspect, which could be described in a written account or with photographs, but is hard to interpret in terms of its effect on behaviour. A video would catch everything and provide back-up data, but working the equipment might distract from the ability to observe in the here and now. One could count the people: determining the number of men and women, their age, how they are dressed, their demeanour. There might be nothing going on or a burst of activity, so where would one focus? Impressions would need to be recorded, as well as the 'facts' of who is going in and out.
- When to observe? Maybe an exercise such as this is ideal for a group project. Each person can then record whatever they want and see what each has seen in the same place and time, but perhaps from different angles (from the dress circle, the stalls, in the wings …). It would also be possible to repeat this on several occasions at the same or different times.
- How should we analyse the results? What do the observations tell us about the culture of this organization – or rather the organization in its context, with the entrance being at the boundary (physically) between the organization and its environment? An inductive, impressionistic approach to interpretation would probably give some idea about the different ways of thinking about organization culture, but, without real rigour, it is rather like a wet-finger test of the wind. It could be made more systematic, by, for example, taking Schein's work on organization culture (1985), and using the categories that he provides as the basis for an interpretation of the data. This could lead to a keener awareness of the 'reality' of the lived culture as

Continued

expressed in such observable phenomena as the language, ceremonies, rituals and norms (Schein's 'artefacts'). However, some artefacts are physical, some more symbolic; some are visible, others not. Gaining access to the meaning of such things to organizational members would entail talking with some of them, in order to get an 'insider' perspective that might help interpretation of what we had observed. Interesting as this might be, it would be moving beyond the original, time-limited observation exercise. It would take the research into new territory, with its own issues of data collection and analysis.

Case Study 3 is an account of a collaborative research project with managers and leaders in the UK public services, who were participating in a postgraduate programme, and in which a mask was used to generate data. It was a deceptively simple exercise that proved to be remarkably effective, as illustrated by a participant's account of the experience below.

At this point, it is worth recalling the ethical issues that arise in the use of creative methods in organizational research (discussed in Chapter 2). We were aware that when tutors initiate a collaborative research event in the classroom, students might feel pressurized to participate in the process because of the asymmetrical power relationship between tutors and students. Our way of addressing this was to discuss the issue openly with the participants, emphasizing that participation in the exercise was entirely voluntary. The inquiry proceeded on the basis of informed consent by all participants, with students and staff mutually interested in a critical inquiry into the thinking and practices associated with our own experiences and practices in service provision – the service–user relationships. The research aimed to explore the assumption that interaction between service providers and users, can be affected by habitual practice, expectations and projections, and that these ritualised and surface exchanges between them could inhibit the expression of their authentic voices and as a result potentially reduce the effectiveness of the service provision. It was to get beneath the surface that we chose the use of masks as a research method to generate data that are complex, not easily accessed, and emotionally charged.

Case study 3: masks and voice

To set the research project in motion, we invited people to, in their minds, convert the classroom into 'live' theatre, with a chair at one end of the room representing the stage, and with the research participants – 15 students and three members of staff – sitting at the other end. It was as if the entire group was a Greek chorus. Members of this chorus could stand up; go to the focal chair;

say something; and then return to their own place, moving at will on to (and off) the stage, as it were, and into (and out of) the spotlight. The intention was to access the 'hidden' voice of the community and public service users, which we all knew both in our professional roles as service providers, and in our 'ordinary' roles as citizens, and therefore also as service users.

The key extra ingredient was the mask: a blank mask was placed on the focal chair, so that the person choosing to sit there could hold it in front of their face as she or he responded to the question: 'How is the voice of this community heard?' Having said what they wanted to say, they would then place the mask back on the seat of the chair and return to their own chair.

We chose a featureless mask, (see Figure 7.4) in the hope that its lack of 'personality' would allow participants to express more subdued or 'forgotten'

Continued

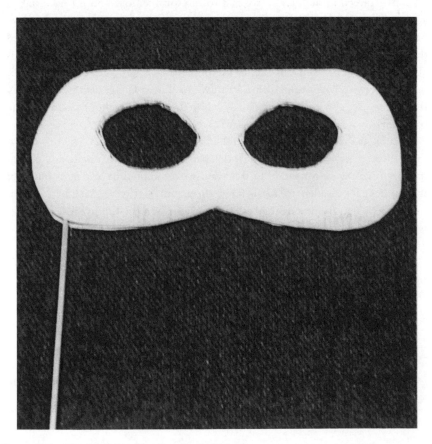

Figure 7.4   The Mask Used in Case Study 3

voices from their experience; to allow them to give expression to many voices; and also to 'take in' the impact of sounds which might be amplified and come alive through the mask's anonymous *persona*.

The use of this mask certainly had a significant impact on the 'voices' that were accessed. At first – and almost immediately – one person came to the chair, and then another, and another. The speed of movement to and fro quickened, with everyone drawn to the chair – even the staff. Everyone came to the chair at least once, most more than once, and some came several times. There was much movement, an air of animation, and there were many voices.

We continued until everyone had had their say, and then the image of the theatre was dissolved, and we returned to a discussion-group format. With the help of the mask, rich and complex data had been generated in the matrix of the group, and now we turned to analysis.

In retrospect, we regretted the fact that we did not make an audio- or video-recording of the event. Because we were participants as well as leaders of the session – 'directing the play' – we had to rely on memory and on notes taken at the time, with the result that some of the richness of the data might have been lost. It was difficult to remember both the content of what was said and the overall drama of the experience. Nonetheless, the exercise revealed to us all the potential of even this simple use of a mask to generate data that might never otherwise have surfaced for scrutiny. In this case, the data generated by the group were also captured and analysed by the group – rather than just by the researchers.

As soon as the mask 'play' had finished, each participant was asked to take a moment on their own to think about what had happened, and to write down what had been significant for them. In this way, we attempted to 'catch' as much of the moment as possible – to freeze-frame the action, as it were. Each person then shared their 'significant experiences' in the group, and their individual responses were recorded on a flip-chart. This gave us a list that offered an additional dimension to what had been said during the exercise itself. It also began to give a means of assessing which aspects of the raw data were perceived to be the most significant.

The following extracts give a flavour of this stage of the analysis:

- 'When I spoke from behind the mask, all I could hear was my own voice. Everyone was quiet, listening. I could hear the sound of my voice getting stronger – it was empowering!'
- 'It was as if our [service-] users were 'with us', even 'inside us', as we put the mask to our faces'.

The next part of the analysis was to ask individuals what it was that had made their 'significant experiences' significant: what were the thoughts and feelings that the experience raised for them? As individuals worked through their own data, they drew out the meaning that the data held for them. As a result, the group was able to compare and contrast the individual experiences, in order to trace connections and emerging patterns.

The next stage of the analysis was for the group to compare and contrast the experience of the exercise with their experience at work; that is, to make connections and parallels between the participants' experiences in the research exercise and those that they have at work in the role of service-providers to other service-users. The question for critical reflection was: 'How did the experience of 'voice' in *this* inquiry compare with that of the community/ies that you work with in your organizations?'

In terms of the initial findings that emerged from this process described in case study 3, the first thing that we noted was that participation using the mask was greater than normal, and that the contributions were qualitatively different. The mask seemed to liberate people to speak their mind plainly (as users, patients, citizens, etc.) and in some cases forcibly. Although the explicit values within the classroom are for inclusion and the contribution of each person, the experience was that participation was not equal. And yet, in the research exercise, the use of the mask had produced unexpectedly wider participation and inclusion. This challenged the group to question the relationship between the values that we express and how we behave in practice, and to consider questions such as: 'What were the resistances and blockages to participation and what freed it up'? and, 'What are the implications for the workplace?'

The use of group discussion in the analysis made us focus attention on the assumptions, values and theories that might be at work shaping participation in different contexts: the research exercise, the classroom and the workplace. Our roles in this stage of analysis as initiators of the research process were to manage the process of group analysis and keep the discussion focused on the aim. Group members were encouraged to interpret the experience of this research exercise and to invite members to reflect on the theories that they held about participation, and the extent to which these theories were applied in different arenas of practice. Figure 7.5 represents the relationship between the theory of participation espoused and practised in different settings.

The story that follows is one participant's account of the impact that the research exercise had on him.

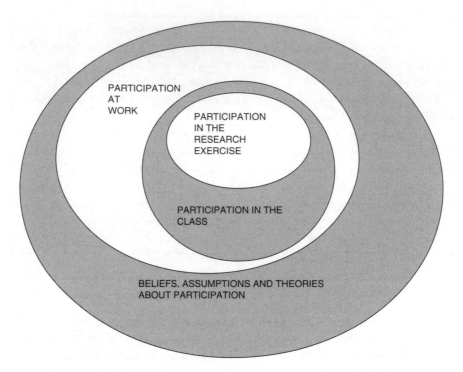

Figure 7.5   Relating the Experience of Participation in the Research Exercise to Theory and Practice in Other Areas

Masks and voice: a participant's story

There was the chair in front of us, with an androgynous mask lying on it. Phil had invited us to go to the chair, pick up the mask, and speak from the point of view of a user of public services. I didn't have the nerve to go first, and was mightily relieved when someone else did. This wasn't going to work, was it? How do you get research data from this? But it was uncanny, and strangely moving. As people spoke through the mask, they did seem to find a voice that wasn't 'theirs'. I particularly remember Julie, who was pretty well in (real) tears behind the mask as 'she' (in the role of an elderly patient in a care institution) bemoaned the fact that no one was listening to her: 'Why can't you just listen to what I'm saying? ... Please! ... I need you to see what I'm going through ...' Julie herself seemed stunned at what had been evoked in her through this apparently simple act.

It was time for me to have a go! I had no idea what I was going to say when I got there, but somehow this felt alright. As I looked out awkwardly from behind the mask, I recollected suddenly an occasion a few years ago when a user (a student – I'm a lecturer) was incredibly angry with me because, as he had put it, he hadn't paid all this money to be asked what he thought. He was in a complete rage. He had paid to hear from experts (including me!). He just wanted the answers, not more questions. My experience behind the mask was uncanny. Somehow it unleashed this 'user's' anger, and I 'took on' that anger as I expressed what he had said to me those years before. Clearly the incident had made a deep impact on me, because I remember returning to my seat slightly embarrassed at the vehemence with which I had expressed this student's anger. It also made me remember my own angry reaction to him, and to think about what was going on in the staff/student relationship at that time.

I remember a lot from those few seconds that I was in the chair, holding the mask up to my face. I remember to this day what it was like to put a physical, symbolic device between my face and the rest of the group. There was something liberating about it, giving a kind of permission to remember and to express something that had been locked away. It was as if our users were 'with us', even 'inside us', and as we put the mask to our faces we took on their roles and acted them out. I think all of us who got into the process were touched somehow by the characters that we portrayed. And I just don't think it would have been possible without the mask.

It is worth noting that there were three further stages to the processing of the data from this research exercise:

1. Students were able to reflect individually on the exercise in their assignments for the module. Many chose to do so – and some also used it subsequently as the basis for the design of their dissertations.
2. Some took the learning back into their workplace and were able to implement changes as a result.
3. For staff, the experience contributed to the development of thinking around leadership in the public sector (Kirk, 2003; Kirk and Shutte, 2004)

CONCLUSION

Masks and theatre can provide powerful metaphors for use in research. The power comes from the way in which these metaphors can help to focus attention on stage and *persona*, on masks and the mask-wearer-in-role. Theatre needs an audience: it is when they have taken their seats, the curtain is raised and the action begins on stage, that people really look and listen. And this is what research is about: *really looking* and *really listening*. Without this, many of the dramas, tragedies and comedies played out in everyday life can go unnoticed.

So the lens of mask and theatre may help the researcher to see in a different way, and can make the action and the motivation of the 'players' more visible. In case studies 1 and 3 above, it was particularly important that the 'actors' and mask-wearers were invited to be the audience in their own play, to critique it, review it, and learn from it. Case study 2, however, did not demand this level of involvement. Our intention in choosing these case studies has been to show that this approach offers possibilities at several levels of complexity.

Ethical considerations are important in all research (Chapter 2). They need special attention in relation to research using theatre and masks, because the approach is somewhat unusual. Without some prior discussion and explanation, research participants may give consent too readily, thinking this is 'just play'. Case study 3, however, demonstrates the potential of such 'play': it can take people off guard and, by reducing inhibitions, can generate unexpected emotions. Hamlet recognized this possibility: 'The play's the thing/ Wherein I'll catch the conscience of the king.' As researchers, we therefore need to be clear about how we are going to use the method, and, if necessary, how to explain it to participants. Only if we can achieve this clarity can informed consent be secured in a proper and meaningful way.

Our hope is that this chapter will have opened up the possibilities and potential of the 'theatre and mask' metaphor in research, and that it provides a stimulus for organizational and management researchers to think about whether their research projects lend themselves to the use of theatre or masks in some way or in some part.

DISCUSSION QUESTIONS

1. 'Man is least himself when he talks in his own person. Give him a mask and he will tell the truth.' (Oscar Wilde). How may masks enable research participants to voice their feelings and experiences?
2. What are the theatrical origins of the concept of *role*?
3. How do the notions or metaphors of *costume, mask, role, stage, script, performance* apply to your role and/or organization?
4. What are the special ethical matters to be considered when using masks and theatre in organizational research?

FURTHER READING

Iain Mangham (1995a) provides a critique of Alasdair MacIntyre's (1985) work, which presents the idea of 'characters' on the organizational 'stage'. The notion explored is that in drama 'there are a stock of 'characters' immediately recognized by the audience, and that such characters partially define the possibilities of plot and action'. The transfer of this idea to the organization is developed in this paper, and in particular the role of 'manager', 'that central character of the modern social drama.' (pp. 182, 188).

Mangham (1995b) looks at conversations between people in organizations and analyses them as 'scripts', which to him indicate the possibility of routinized responses between individuals. Through the analysis the participants 'learned to see how patterns of behaviour were triggered by particular ways of talking and they learned how to talk differently'. He says, 'They talked themselves a new script and they talked themselves into performing it.' (p. 511).

In addition, Oswick *et al.* (2003) consider dramaturgy as a means of exploring organizational contexts. They discuss the interplay between fiction and reality as features of drama and organizational life. Finally, they discuss an approach that they call 'dialogical scripting' to construct scripts for theatrical plays based on real organizational events.

MacIntyre, A. (1985) *After Virtue: A Study in Moral Theory* (Second edition), London: Duckworth

Mangham, I. (1995a) 'MacIntyre and the Manager', *Organization*, Vol. 2, No. 2: 181–204

Mangham, I. (1995b) 'Scripts, Talk and Double Talk', *Management Learning*, Vol. 26, No. 4: 493–511

Oswick, C., Mangham, I., Keenoy, T., Grant, D. and Anthony, P. (2003) 'Dramaturgy, dialogue and organizing', in S. Linstead (Ed.) *Text/Work: Representing Organization and Organizing Representation*, London: Routledge, 219–229

REFLECTIONS

CHAPTER 8

REFLECTIONS

Margaret Page and Mike Broussine

OVERVIEW

- **Critical reflections on creative methods in management and organizational research**
- **Meeting the challenge of using creative methods – legitimacy**
- **A research supervisor's story – is the use of art in a dissertation academically rigorous?**
- **Epistemologies that affirm multiple ways of knowing**
- **Meeting the challenge of using creative methods – validity**
- **Conclusion**
- **Discussion questions**
- **Further reading**

CRITICAL REFLECTIONS ON CREATIVE METHODS IN MANAGEMENT AND ORGANIZATIONAL RESEARCH

This book has set out to acquaint the management and organizational researcher with an emerging tradition and developing practice in organizational research where creative methods are used to understand more about people's experiences of organizations and systems. We have framed our exploration in ways that aim to generate confidence in employing these methods, while holding a critical awareness about their pros and cons and about oneself in the process. Our view is that creative organizational research methods have come some way since Braud and Anderson asserted back in 1998 that:

> Many of the most significant and exciting life events and extraordinary experiences – moments of clarity, illumination, and healing – have been systematically excluded from conventional research, along with the ways of recognizing and encouraging these exceptional experiences. Such unfortunate exclusions, through which we deprive ourselves of new and nourishing forms of knowledge and experience, are attributable to the narrowness of conventional conceptualizations of research and of the appropriate methods for its conduct.
>
> (Braud and Anderson, 1998, p. 3)

Hopefully, the earlier Chapters of this book have contributed to understanding of creative research methods, both through critical reflections on our own research practices, and by reviewing the stories, reflections and experiences of dissertation or doctoral students and management and organizational researchers who have used them. We have argued that creative forms of inquiry, set within a collaborative relationship with research participants, can make a significant contribution to the repertoire of qualitative and interpretive methodologies. They can give us ways in which to access the new and nourishing forms of knowledge and experience that Braud and Anderson speak of. However, as we have maintained throughout, creative methods in organizational research pose some special challenges, and, in this final Chapter, we reflect on what we have learned about these challenges and how the critically aware researcher can address them. Back in Chapter 2, we promised that we would reflect further about the methods' legitimacy and validity once we had completed our journey of learning. Two related questions have emerged from these reflections, and these are offered as organizing themes that might be useful for researchers who wish to develop a creative approach in their research practice. These questions are:

- How can the creative researcher defend the *legitimacy* of creative methods?
- How can the creative researcher affirm the *validity* of creative methods?

These challenges enable us to frame an overall critical review of the methods. Our collective endeavour in this book has been, above all, to encourage the management and organizational researcher to use creative methods, and we are aware that this mission derives from a commitment and enthusiasm that has emerged from our experiences of using them, both in our own research, and in observing how they have been used to good effect by research students and other researchers. There is a need, therefore, to take stock – to bring together a critical reflection about the use of these methods in organizational research while not losing sight of the benefits that have been extolled throughout this book. In the language of Chapter 2, we need to be aware of the seductive qualities of creative methods, and adopt a healthy scepticism that enables us to achieve good-quality creative research.

MEETING THE CHALLENGE OF USING CREATIVE METHODS – LEGITIMACY

A challenge that faces the creative organizational researcher is the need to defend the *legitimacy* of creative methods. The proposal to use these methods may confront traditional notions of what it is to be a researcher, and about the nature of knowledge itself. As we discussed in Chapter 1, in some circumstances, particularly in systems where there is a strong adherence to positivist notions of what research is, creative methods may be vulnerable to accusations that they do not constitute 'real research'.

Our interest in using creative methods can be set within a wider context, i.e. the dual quest of introducing creativity in the endeavour of learning more about management and organizations, and in order to enable organizations to survive and thrive in a competitive global environment (Henry, 2006). However, the draw towards reliance on rational thinking and analysis among managers can be strong. Thus, Amabile (2006) discusses the ways in which creativity may be crushed unintentionally in organizations because of the pursuit to maximize business imperatives such as productivity and control, and she shows how it may be possible to develop circumstances in which creativity can flourish while business imperatives are attended to. Weick (2003) argues that business strategy requires us to call on both our analytical and creative capacities. She feels that while there are plenty of materials that teach students about the analytical characteristics of strategy-making, creative materials are scarce, and she presents a way in which instructors can encourage creative thinking in their business strategy courses by using materials and exercises based on metaphor. Wilson and Stokes (2005) explore the key ingredients of creative entrepreneurial work, including: the combination of individualistic values with collaborative working; being members of a wider creative community; and a blurring of the demarcation line between work and non-work – i.e. that many entrepreneurs say that their best ideas come to them when they are not at work. And Sadler-Smith (2004) explores the questions of whether effective managerial action is better served by 'rational analysis' or 'creative intuition', and of whether managers' decision-making styles actually have an effect on the performance of small and medium-sized enterprises. Sadler-Smith's research has led him to query the pre-eminence of the rational paradigm in management thinking, and he suggests that intuition may be a habitual characteristic of successful entrepreneurs.

In our research with managers, we sometimes invite participants to pick a postcard and then to use it to explore the qualities of their relationship to their organization (this process was discussed briefly in Chapter 4). We encourage them to act on intuition, to be free-associative in exploring how they relate to the picture they have chosen, and to set aside *post hoc* rationalizations or explanations. We ask them to step back from the rationalist thinking that can sometimes predominate in their organizations' cultures, and to set aside their organizational role masks in order to take up roles as research participants and inquirers. This requires us, as leaders or initiators of research, sometimes to brave their scepticism about this not being 'real research'. By extension, some of us may think privately that in using these methods we are not 'real academics' or 'real researchers'. As we saw in Chapter 1, this may well extend to colleagues, examiners and organizational sponsors.

Researchers are required to legitimate knowledge claims by demonstrating how research meets its criteria for rigour. Legitimation of the use of creative research methodology is important both for established academics and for new researchers and research. In the story that follows, we explore this issue of legitimacy as it arose in our work with a dissertation student.

A research supervisor's story – is the use of art in a dissertation academically rigorous?

A dissertation student was in the final stages of her writing up. In a supervision session, I noticed that discussion had become flat and lifeless. The student seemed exhausted and disconnected from the data she had collected from interviews with her staff, and this was reflected in her draft analysis, which seemed empty and lacking in focus. I was reminded of how much my student had struggled with the invitation to bring her subjectivity into the text. While she might wish to take up the invitation, and did so in discussion, to do so in her written text was experienced by her as countercultural, both within the performance culture of the health service where she worked, and in relation to the positivist notion of academic knowledge that she held.

A breakthrough happened when the student mentioned that she had recently enjoyed visiting an art exhibition. I remembered my own enjoyment of the same exhibition, and suggested that she allow herself to think about her research while looking at her favourite paintings. This brought the discussion to life, and a few weeks later I received a postcard from the student, from an art exhibition, saying that she had experienced a breakthrough while looking at the exhibits. When her draft dissertation arrived, I saw that it now contained a lively and coherent analysis of the complex data that she had collected, and that within the text the student had inserted pictures to illuminate themes that had emerged from her analysis.

In the next supervision session, I congratulated the student. But, to my surprise, the student seemed sceptical. In discussion she spoke about how the process of allowing herself to muse and reflect on the paintings had helped her to find a way

---

in to the data. However, it was hard for her to believe in the academic rigour and quality of the text that she had produced. I could see that my authority as an academic was not enough to affirm the legitimacy of her work: she felt she needed to reference additional external sources so that she could begin to feel that the academic legitimacy of her work could be demonstrated.

Epistemologies that affirm multiple ways of knowing, and that challenge the hegemony of propositional knowledge within the academy and practical knowledge within organizations, have been developed within a variety of post-positivist, feminist and action-research traditions (e.g. Goldberger *et al.*, 1996; Reason and Bradbury, 2001). All of these play an important role in legitimating creative research and in broadening the scope of ways that academics take up their supervisory roles in relation to research students.

One such epistemology is offered by Heron's four modes of knowing (Heron, 1971), summarized later by Reason (2001) – see the box below. Within this epistemology, propositional, or cognitive, intellectual knowledge is the mode favoured by the academy, while presentational, experiential and practical knowing co-exist and are equally important in sense-making. It may be obvious to say that presentational knowledge is what we know, but such knowledge may not always be verbally or consciously articulated, or it may be expressed in constrained ways. It is what is literally 'presented' in its creative form – whether it is a story, poem, picture, bodily expression or music. Practical knowledge is what we know by doing, and experiential is what we know through direct encounter, or experience.

Four ways of knowing

Knowing will be more valid – richer, deeper, more true to life and more useful – if these four ways of knowing are congruent with each other: if our knowing is grounded in our experience; expressed through our stories and images; understood through theories which make sense to us; and expressed in worthwhile action in our lives.

- *Experiential knowing* is through direct face-to-face encounter with a person, place or thing; it is knowing through empathy and resonance; and precedes any form of expression or communication.
- *Presentational knowing* emerges from experiential knowing, and provides its first expression through forms of imagery such as poetry and stories, drawing, sculpture, movement, dance and so on.

Continued

> • *Propositional knowing* is knowing 'about' something, through ideas and theories, and is expressed in abstract language or mathematics.
> • *Practical knowing* is knowing 'how to' do something, and is expressed in a skill, knack or competence.
>
> (Reason, 2001, pp. 184–185)

It is useful in addition to set alongside Heron's four ways of knowing the ideas proposed by Nonaka and Toyama (2003), who sought to explain the interaction between tacit and explicit knowledge. Their ideas are relevant because they seek to explain the relationship between invisible and visible knowledge, and we have argued regularly through this book how creative research methods may enable us to access empirical material that is not always accessible through conventional methodologies. Nonaka and Toyama argue that we enact our daily actions with two main levels of consciousness – practical and discursive. Our discursive consciousness refers to more conscious and therefore more explicitly theoretical knowing, while practical consciousness refers to the level of our lives that we do not really think or theorize about. In that sense, we can say that tacit knowledge is produced by our practical consciousness, and explicit knowledge is produced by our discursive consciousness. Thus, the creative researcher can address the legitimacy challenge by developing a capacity and an authority to work with research approaches that involve accessing and working with multiple ways of knowing, to include both 'invisible' as well as 'visible' ways of knowing. We have discussed such ways throughout this book. Beeby and Simpson, in Chapter 3, showed how their procedure for creative dialogue incorporates multiple methods for accessing experiential data; Broussine, in Chapter 4, demonstrated how the use of drawings and art in research accesses a range of types of empirical materials (see especially Figure 4.10); Simpson, in Chapter 5, discussed how stories invariably consist of different layers and elements that the researcher needs to be aware of as he or she analyses them; Grisoni, in Chapter 6, emphasized the fact that a major strength of using poetry in organizational research is precisely the fact that the process uncovers the possibility of multiple interpretations; and Kirk and French, in Chapter 7, show how the metaphors of theatre and masks can offer insights at several levels of complexity.

In the research supervisor's story on page 156, art became a means for the dissertation student to access the meaning of her research, through experiential knowing, and to present it as a dimension of her sense-making, thereby illustrating and supporting her analysis. The four modes of knowing enabled her to affirm the legitimacy of her study, which might otherwise have remained specific to the relationship formed between the supervisor and the student, and therefore private, invisible and unnamed within the research text. Invisibility within the text would have reproduced the 'disappearing' of emotional and lived experience within organizational life that creative methods seek to reintroduce.

MEETING THE CHALLENGE OF USING CREATIVE
METHODS – VALIDITY

We argued in our introduction that the management and organizational researcher's aim in using creative methods is to understand more about the affective domain in organizational life, whether directly communicated in creative encounters with organizational researchers, or more indirectly through metaphorical and/or symbolic material. This depth includes possibilities of accessing tacit, unstated, unacknowledged, unconscious and 'invisible' material. The second challenge for the organizational researcher who seeks to use creative methods, is to address the question of *validity*. Heron (1971) and Reason's (2001), and Nonaka and Toyama's (2003) frameworks offer ways of naming different forms of knowing, and we explore now how the concept of 'congruence' between them may be seen as a basis for research validity. From this perspective, creative research methods may be understood as a means of exploring congruence or dissonance between different forms of knowing. In large measure, this challenge surrounds an important question concerning validity – how can we be sure that each method is allowing truly hidden or latent knowledge or phenomena to surface; or is it merely presenting overt or explicit knowledge in a different form – pictures, poems, etc. – rather than words or numbers? Or, as we put it in Chapter 2, is the method giving an insight into the authentic lived experience in the social system being investigated, or is it what the participant wants the researcher to hear?

The preceding Chapters, each exploring the potential use of a specific method, have shown how a 'rich' insight can be gained by both research participants and the researcher by accessing different forms of knowing through creative means. For example, Chapter 3 discussed how learning maps used in creative dialogue were a source of alternative perspectives, and how, through them, new and different meanings emerged in each of the participants' stories. Chapter 4 emphasized that the data emerging from the use of art are both multifaceted and interrelated, for example the emotional dimensions of an experience (experiential knowing) may be expressed by an individual participant through the production of a drawing (presentational knowing), and theorized through sense-making with the researcher and other participants (propositional knowing). The findings may well challenge predominant discourses and accounts of organizational life and management processes. The 'dissonance ' between the experiences expressed through creative processes including story-telling, may thus enable forms of knowledge about dimensions of organizational life to emerge that were previously hidden from view, and to allow silent voices to emerge.

Seeking to work with these different forms of knowing can represent a significant challenge to management and organizational researchers and participants, and together we have explored the nature of these challenges as we have gone along. For example, in Chapter 4 we recounted the incident of the 'reluctant drawer' (Figure 4.4) where a senior manager at first refused to participate in the research process. In Chapter 5, we problematized the story as a creative research method by suggesting that even as research participants 'tell it as it is', they will be constrained by the language available to them within prevailing discourses. In Chapter 6, we pointed to the potential for challenge within researcher–participant relationships when participants express through poetry thoughts, feelings and emotions that hitherto were well-guarded within organizational cultures where such expression might make them vulnerable. Inquiry or research processes that involve organizational members in a collaborative relationship with the researcher, can give rise to tensions between the ways that they might normally take up their roles in contexts where practical or propositional knowing are privileged and emphasized. Organizations, like individuals, can resist innovation by suppressing knowledge of certain dimensions of experience from organizational life.

Such challenges raise both ethical and political questions concerning participant vulnerability within the research process because predominant ways of knowing and discourses can be challenged through the research process. Engaging creatively with these challenges requires the researcher to maintain a good capacity for awareness (in the terms of Chapter 2), and a willingness to engage with such issues with sensitivity within a well-formed researcher–participant relationship.

Even with permission and encouragement to do so, participants may have difficulty recognizing organizational learning through what is evoked by creative research methods. It is as if the separation between propositional and other forms of knowing is so powerful in Western culture that whole dimensions of our experience are 'disappeared' as we move between different modes of knowing. To 'hold on to' these hidden dimensions, frameworks are needed within which the work of integration can take place. This work of integration is necessarily a political act, and as such carries its own risks.

Thus, multiple forms of knowing need to be worked with in the relationship between the researcher and the participant. The researcher will need to hold an awareness of the potential for movement and insight in moving from one mode of knowing to another, and for congruence and dissonance to emerge between different forms of knowledge that are arrived at in these different modes. Therein, we believe, lies the claim to validity. Creative methods offer a variety of different methods for accessing dimensions of experiential knowing that are not represented in predominant presentational forms, and they offer processes of sense-making for generating new propositional and practical knowing.

Creative methods – inviting research participants to produce a drawing, to tell their story, engage in creative dialogue or to explore their experience through masks or poetry – offer ways of exploring, making sense of, and, in the language of Chapter 1, giving voice to, aspects of experience that might not figure within the supposed 'givens' of day-to-day organizational life.

CONCLUSION

Our hope is that we have illustrated how poetry, the visual arts, drama, stories and creative dialogue can offer us avenues through which we may understand more about the rich and complex human experience in organizations. We have shown how such methods used in research in and with organizations can enable organizational members to access this richness and complexity, and thus make them available to organizational members and researchers. This Chapter has discussed how the management researcher or organizational researcher can argue the legitimacy and validity of the methods. We also believe that creative methods are not simply about enabling others – research participants – to access more hidden or tacit aspects of their experience. In doing so, they also touch the researcher, enabling her or him to access dimensions of knowing and experience that enrich and add complexity and focus to his or her inquiry and sense-making capacities.

Back in our introduction, we mentioned that the researcher could get a 'buzz' out of doing research. Etherington (2004), in reflecting on the use of art as a mode of inquiry, felt that creative depictions:

> … give data a life and dimension beyond that reached by the written word alone …[and] convey the visual, intellectually, bodily and emotional qualities of the experiences being studied.
>
> (Etherington, 2004, p. 150)

We suggest that the management- and organizational researcher who employs creative methods in a critically aware way will, together with research participants, often be surprised by and delighted at how research participants can respond to the offer to move outside the usual frames of knowing to tap into aspects of their rich and complex human experience in organizations. As Marcel Proust put it in *À la Recherche du Temps perdu* (1913–27):

> La vraie découverte ne consiste pas à chercher de nouveaux paysages mais à changer de regard.

…The real voyage of discovery is not in seeking new landscapes but in having new eyes.

DISCUSSION QUESTIONS

1. What arguments would you put forward to demonstrate that creative methods can constitute legitimate management or organizational research?

Continued

2. How can the idea of 'dissonance' help us understand how creative methods may enable different forms of knowing about organizational experience to emerge that were previously hidden from view?
3. How would you describe your motives for, or attraction to, creative methods in management or organizational research?
4. Can you express your answer to question 3 above in a drawing, as a poem, a story and/or as a piece of theatre?

FURTHER READING

In order to gain an understanding of a range of approaches to looking at creativity in management, the reader is recommended to consult Jane Henry's edited book. She argues that, in order to survive, organizations need to be continuously creative and innovative, and the principal idea of the book is to examine the processes that underpin creative management.

The 'Concise Adair' (Adair, 2004) book on creativity and innovation provides an accessible introduction to creativity and creative thinking by John Adair. This short book sets out, among other things, to develop our understanding of the creative process; to overcome barriers to having new ideas and creative thoughts; to enlarge our parameters of vision and information; and to increase our tolerance for uncertainty and doubt.

Finally, Tony Proctor's 1999 book offers a comprehensive account of the importance of creativity to business, the blocks to creativity, and of some theories concerning creativity and creative problem-solving processes. It also devotes a Chapter each to a range of creative problem-solving techniques, such as morpho-logical analysis, brainstorming and lateral thinking.

Adair, J. (2004) *Concise Adair on Creativity and Innovation*, London: Thorogood
Henry, J. (Ed.) (2006) *Creative Management and Development* (Third edition), London: Sage Publications
Proctor, T. (1999) *Creative Problem Solving for Managers*, London: Routledge

REFERENCES

Alexander, B.K. (2005) 'Performance Ethnography: the Reenacting and Inciting of Culture', in Denzin, N.K. and Lincoln, Y.S. (Eds) (2005) *The Sage Handbook of Qualitative Research* (Third edition), Thousand Oaks, CA: Sage Publications, pp. 411–441

Alvesson, M. and Deetz, S. (2000) *Doing Critical Management Research*, London: Sage Publications

Amabile, T. (2006) 'How to Kill Creativity', in J. Henry (Ed.) (2006) *Creative Management and Development*, London: Sage Publications, pp. 18–24

Antonacopoulou, E.P. and Bento, R.F. (2004) 'Methods of 'Learning Leadership': Taught and Experiential', in J. Storey (Ed.) *Leadership in Organizations – Current Issues and Key Trends*, Abingdon: Routledge: 81–102

Averill, J.R. (1990) 'Inner Feelings, Works of the Flesh, the Beast Within, Diseases of the Mind, Driving Force, and Putting on a Show: Six Metaphors of Emotion and Their Theoretical Extensions', in D.E. Leary (Ed.) *Metaphors in the History of Psychology*, Cambridge: Cambridge University Press

Bakhtin, M.M. (1986) *Speech Genres and Other Late Essays*. Emerson, C. and Holquist, M. (Eds), McGee, V.W. (Trans.), Austin, TX: University of Texas Press

Barry, D. and Elmes, M. (1997) 'Strategy Retold: Toward a Narrative View of Strategic Discourse', *Academy of Management Review*, Vol. 22, No. 2: 429–452

Beeby, M. and Booth, C. (2000) 'Networks and Inter-organisational Learning: a Critical Review', *The Learning Organisation: An International Journal*, Vol. 7, No. 2: 75–88

Beeby, M., Cowley, P., McLellan, P., Thorne, N. and Tomlinson, P. (2002) 'Mapping Dialogue for Local Government', *Local Governance*, Vol. 28, No. 3: 179–190

Berne, E. (1970) *Games People Play: the Psychology of Human Relationships*, Harmondsworth: Penguin

Blumberg, A. and Golembiewski, R.T. (1976) *Learning and Change in Groups*, Harmondsworth: Penguin

Bochner, A.P. and Ellis, C. (2003) 'An Introduction to the Arts and Narrative Research: Art as Inquiry', *Qualitative Inquiry*, Vol. 9, No. 4: 506–514

Boje, D.M. (1991) 'The Storytelling Organization: a Study of Story Performance in an Office-Supply-Firm', *Administrative Science Quarterly*, Vol. 36, No. 3: 106–126

Boje, D.M., Luhman, J.T. and Cunliffe, A.L. (2003) 'A Dialectic Perspective on the Organization Theatre Metaphor', *American Communication Journal*, Vol. 6, No. 2, Winter 2003, accessed 2 October 2007, http://www.acjournal.org/holdings/vol6/iss2/articles/boje.pdf

Braud, W. and Anderson, R. (1998) *Transpersonal Research Methods for the Social Sciences*, London: Sage Publications

Brearley, L. (2000) 'Exploring the creative voice in an academic context', *The Qualitative Report*, Vol. 5, No. 3/4, accessed 1 October 2007, from http://www.nova.edu/ssss/QR/QR5-3/brearley.html

Brewerton, P. and Millward, J. (2001) *Organizational Research Methods – A Guide for Students and Researchers*, London: Sage Publications

Brice Heath, S. (2000) 'Making Learning Work', The Encyclopedia of Informal Education, http://www.infed.org/enterprise/briceheath_making_learning_work.htm. First published in *After School Matters*, Vol. 1, No. 1: 33–45

Briskin, A. (1998) *Stirring of the Soul in the Workplace*, San Francisco, CA: Berrett-Koehler

Broussine, M. and Fox, P. (2003) 'The Politics of Researching Gender in Organisations', *Management Research News*, Vol. 26, No. 8: 27–37

Broussine, M. and Vince, R. (1995) 'Working with Metaphor Towards Organizational Change', in C. Oswick and D. Grant (Eds), *Organization Development: Metaphorical Explorations*, London: Pitman, 57–72

Bruner, J. (1990) *Acts of Meaning*, Cambridge, MA: Harvard University Press

Burke, W.W. (1992) 'Metaphors to Consult By', *Group and Organization Management*, Vol. 17, No. 3: 255–259

Canham, H. and Satyamurti, C. (2003) *Acquainted With the Night*, London: Karnac Books

Chaplin, E. (1994) *Sociology and Visual Representation*, London: Routledge

Chell, E. (2004) 'Critical Incident Technique', in C. Cassell and G. Symon (Eds), *Essential Guides to Qualitative Methods in Organizational Research*, London: Sage Publications, pp. 45–60

Clandinin, D.J. and Connelly, F.M. (1994) 'Personal Experience Methods', in N.K. Denzin and Y.S. Lincoln (Eds), *Handbook of Qualitative Research*, London: Sage Publications, pp. 413–427

Cortazzi, M. (1993) *Narrative Analysis*, London: Falmer Press

Crotty, M. (1998) *The Foundations of Social Research: Meaning and Perspective in the Research Process*, London: Sage Publications

Csikszentmihalyi, M. and Robinson, R. (1990) *The Art of Seeing: An Interpretation of the Aesthetic*, Malibu, CA: Getty Publishing

Cunliffe, A.L. (2002) 'Social Poetics as Management Inquiry: a Dialogical Approach', *Journal of Management Inquiry*, Vol. 11, No. 2: 128–146

Czarniawska, B. (1998) *A Narrative Approach in Organization Studies*, London: Sage Publications

Czarniawska, B. (1999) *Writing Management: Organization Theory as a Literary Genre*, Oxford: Oxford University Press

Denzin, N.K. (1998) 'The Art and Politics of Interpretation', in N.K. Denzin and Y.S. Lincoln (Eds), *Collecting and Interpreting Qualitative Materials*, London: Sage Publications, pp. 313–344

Denzin, N.K. and Lincoln, Y.S. (2005) *The Sage Handbook of Qualitative Research*, Thousand Oaks, CA: Sage Publications Inc.

Department of Health (2006) *Research Governance Framework for Health and Social Care* (Second edition), London: DoH (available at http://www.dh.gov.uk/en/Publicationsandstatistics/Publications/PublicationsPolicyAndGuidance/DH_4108962)

Dixon, N.M. (1997) 'The Hallways of Learning', *Organizational Dynamics*, Vol. 25, No. 4: 23–34

Dixon, N.M. (1998) *Dialogue at Work: Making Talk Developmental for People and Organizations*, London: Lemos & Crane

Douglas, C. (2002) 'Using Co-operative Inquiry With Black Women Managers: Exploring Possibilities for Moving From Surviving to Thriving', in P. Reason (Ed.) *Special Issue: the Practice of Co-operative Inquiry, Systemic Practice and Action Research*, Vol. 15, No. 3, accessed 2 October 2007, from http://www.bath.ac.uk/carpp/publications/doc_theses_links/c_douglas.html

Easterby-Smith, M. and Malina, D. (1999) 'Cross-cultural Collaborative Research: Toward Reflexivity', *Academy of Management Journal*, Vol. 42, No. 1: 76–86

Easterby-Smith, M., Thorpe, R. and Lowe, A. (2004) *Management Research – An Introduction*, London: Sage Publications

Eden, C. and Huxham, C. (1996) 'Action Research for Management Research', *British Journal of Management*, Vol. 7: 75–86

Edwards, M. (2001) 'Jungian Analytic Art Therapy', in Rubin, J.A. (Ed.) *Approaches to Art Therapy – Theory and Technique*, New York: Brunner-Routledge, pp. 81–94

Eichler, M. (1988) *Nonsexist Research Methods: A Practical Guide*, London: Allen & Unwin

Ellis, C. and Flaherty, M.G. (1992) *Investigating Subjectivity: Research on Lived Experience*, London: Sage Publications

Essex, E.M. and Mainemelis, C. (2002) 'Learning From an Artist About Organizations', *Journal of Management Inquiry*, Vol. 11, No. 2: 148–159

Etherington, K. (2004) *Becoming a Reflexive Researcher – Using Our Selves in Research*, London: Jessica Kingsley

Fineman, S. (Ed.) (1993) *Emotion in Organizations*, London: Sage Publications

Fineman, S. (Ed.) (2000) *Emotion in Organizations* (Second edition), London: Sage Publications

Finley, S. (2003) 'Arts-Based Inquiry in *QI*: Seven Years from Crisis to Guerrilla Warfare', *Qualitative Inquiry*, Vol. 9, No. 2: 281–296

Finley, S. (2005) 'Arts-based Inquiry: Performing Revolutionary Pedagogy', in N.K. Denzin and Y.S. Lincoln (Eds) (2005) *The Sage Handbook of Qualitative Research* (Third edition), Thousand Oaks, CA: Sage Publications, pp. 681–694

French, R. and Simpson, P. (2006) 'Leaders Downplaying Leadership. Researching How Leaders Talk About Themselves', *Leadership*, Vol. 2, No. 4: 469–479

Frost, R. (1973) *Selected Poems*. London: Penguin Books

Furth, G.M. (1988) *The Secret World of Drawings: Healing Through Art*, Boston, MA: Sigo Press

Fyfe, G. and Law, J. (1988) (Eds) *Picturing Power: Visual Depiction and Social Relations, Sociological Review Monograph*, 35, London: Routledge

Gabriel, Y. (1999) *Organizations in Depth*, London: Sage Publications

Geertz, C. (1983) *Local Knowledge: Further Essays in Interpretive Anthropology*, New York: Basic Books

Glesne, C. (1997) 'That Rare Feeling: Re-presenting Research Through Poetic Transcription', *Qualitative Inquiry*, Vol. 3, No. 2: 202–221

Goffman, E. (1959) *The Presentation of Self in Everyday Life*, Garden City, NY: Doubleday

Goldberger, N., Tarule, J., Clinchy, B. and Belenky, M. (1996) *Knowledge, Difference and Power: Essays Inspired by Women's Ways of Knowing*, New York: Basic Books

Grant, D. and Oswick, C. (1996) *Metaphor and Organizations*, London: Sage Publications

Grisoni, L. and Kirk, P. (2006) 'Verse, Voice and Va Va Voom! Illuminating Management Processes Through Poetry', *Management Decision*, Vol. 44, No. 4: 512–525

Guba, E.G. and Lincoln, Y.S. (1989) *Fourth Generation Evaluation*, Thousand Oaks, CA: Sage Publications

Guba, E.G. and Lincoln, Y.S. (2005) 'Paradigmic Controversies, Contradictions, and Emerging Confluences', in N.K. Denzin and Y.S. Lincoln (Eds) (2005) *The Sage Handbook of Qualitative Research* (Third edition), Thousand Oaks, CA: Sage Publications, pp. 191–215

Harper, D. (1998) 'On the Authority of the Image', in N.K. Denzin and Y.S. Lincoln (Eds), *Collecting and Interpreting Qualitative Materials*, Thousand Oaks, CA: Sage Publications, pp. 130–149

Harris Smith, S. (1984) *Masks in Modern Drama*, Berkeley, CA: University of California Press

Harrison, B. (2002) 'Seeing Health and Illness Worlds – Using Visual Methodologies', *Sociology of Health and Illness*, Vol. 24, No. 6: 856–872

Hatch, M.J., Kostera, M. and Koźmiński, A.K. (2005) *Three Faces of Leadership*, Oxford: Blackwell Publishing

Hedley, A. (1997) *The Emperor's New Clothes*, University of the West of England: MBA Dissertation

Henry, J. (2006) *Creative Management and Development* (Third edition), London: Sage Publications

Heron, J. (1971) *Experience and Method: An Inquiry Into the Concept of Experiential Research*, University of Surrey: Human Potential Research Project

Heron, J. and Reason, P. (2001) 'The Practice of Co-operative Inquiry: Research With Rather Than on People', in P. Reason and H. Bradbury (Eds), *Handbook of Action Research: Participative Inquiry and Practice*, London: Sage Publications, pp. 179–188

Hobson, R.F. (1985) *Forms of Feeling: the Heart of Psychotherapy*, New York: Tavistock Publications/Methuen

Hofstede, G. (1991) *Cultures and Organizations: Software of the Mind*, London: McGraw-Hill

Höpfl, H. (1995) 'Improving Customer Service, the Cultivation of Contempt', *Studies in Culture, Organizations and Societies*, Vol. 1, No. 2: 47–63

Isaacs, W.N. (1993) 'Taking Flight: Dialogue, Collective Thinking, and Organizational Learning', *Organizational Dynamics*, Vol. 22: 24–39

James, W. (1957) *The Principles of Psychology*, Volumes 1 and 2, New York: Dover Publications

Jessop, B. (2002) *Governance and Metagovernance: on Reflexivity, Requisite Variety and Requisite Irony*, Lancaster University: Department of Sociology, last accessed 2 October 2007, at http://www.lancs.ac.uk/fass/sociology/papers/jessop-governance-and-metagovernance.pdf

Jung, C.G. (1964) *Man and His Symbols*, London: Aldus

Keeping, C. (2006) *Emotional Aspects of the Professional Identity of Social Workers: A Study of Social Workers Working With Avon and Wiltshire Mental Health Partnership NHS Trust*, Bristol: University of the West of England

Kirk, P. (2003) 'Voice and Leadership', presented to conference *Leadership, Voice and Accountability – Local and Global Perspectives*, Bristol: University of the West of England, 8–10 September

Kirk, P. and Shutte, A. M. (2004) 'Community Leadership Development', *Community Development Journal*, Vol. 39, No. 3: 234–251

Kostera, M. (1997) 'Personal Performatives: Collecting Poetical Definitions of Management', *Organization*, Vol. 4, No. 3: 345–353

Kusenbach, M. (2005) 'News From the Old World: Report of a Conference on Qualitative Social Research in Europe', *Qualitative Sociology*, Vol. 28, No. 1: 117–121

Labov, W. (1972) *Language in the Inner City: Studies in the Black English Vernacular*, Oxford: Basil Blackwell

Labov, W. and Waletzky, J. (1967) 'Narrative Analysis', in J. Helm (Ed.) *Essays on the Verbal and Visual Arts*, Seattle: University of Washington Press, 12–44

Lakoff, G. and Johnson, M. (1980) *Metaphors We Live By*, Chicago, IL: University of Chicago Press

Lawrence, G.W. (Ed.) (1998) *Social Dreaming @ Work*, London: Karnac Books

Levi-Strauss, C. (1963) *Structural Anthropology*, London: Penguin Press

Linstead, S. (2006) 'Exploring Culture With the Radio Ballads: Using Aesthetics to Facilitate Change', *Management Decision*, Vol. 44, No. 4: 474–485

McDougall, J. (1986) *Theatres of the Mind: Illusion and Truth on the Psychoanalytical Stage*, London: Free Association Books

Mair, J.M.M. (1977) 'The Community of Self', in D. Bannister (Ed.) *New Perspectives in Personal Construct Theory*, London: Academic Press, 125–149

Mangham, I.L. (1986) *Power and Performance in Organizations*, Oxford: Basil Blackwell

Mangham, I.L. and Overington, M.A. (1987) *Organizations as Theatre: a Social Psychology of Dramatic Appearances*, Chichester: John Wiley

Marcic, D. (2002) 'Tuning Into the Harmonics of Management', in T. Brown and R. Brown (Eds), *The Encyclopaedia of Management*, London: Bloomsbury Publishing

Marshall, J. and Reason, P. (1998) 'Collaborative and Self-Reflective Forms of Inquiry in Management Research', in J. Burgoyne and M. Reynolds (Eds), *Management Learning: Integrating Perspectives in Theory and Practice*, London: Sage Publications, pp. 226–242

Maylor, H. and Blackmon, K. (2005) *Researching Business and Management*, Basingstoke: Palgrave Macmillan

Mead, G.H. (1934) *Mind, Self and Society*, Chicago, IL: University of Chicago Press

Meyer, A. (1991) 'Visual Data in Organisational Research', *Organisation Science*, Vol. 2, No. 2: 218–236

Mienczakowski, J. and Morgan, S. (2001) 'Ethnodrama: Constructing Participatory, Experiential and Compelling Action Research Through Performance', in P. Reason and H. Bradbury (Eds), *Handbook of Action Research: Participatory Inquiry and Practice*, London: Sage Publications, pp. 219–227

Mitroff, I.I. and Kilmann, R.H. (1975) 'Stories That Managers Tell: a New Tool For Organizational Problem Solving', *Management Review*, Vol. 64, No. 7: 18–28

Morgan, G. (1986, 2006) *Images of Organisation*, London: Sage Publications

Moriarty, S. (2004) 'Visual Semiotics Theory', in K.L. Smith, S.E. Moriarty, G. Barbatsis and K. Kenney (Eds.) *Handbook of Visual Communication: Theory, Methods, and Media*, Mahwah, NJ: Lawrence Erlbaum Associates, pp. 227–241

Mullen, C.A. (2003) 'Guest Editor's Introduction: "A Self-Fashioned Gallery of Aesthetic Practice"', *Qualitative Inquiry*, Vol. 9, No. 2: 165–181

Nonaka, I. and Toyama, R. (2003) 'The Knowledge-Creating Theory Revisited: Knowledge Creation as a Synthesizing Process', *Knowledge Management Research and Practice*, Vol. 1, No. 1: 2–10

Nunley, J., McCarthy, C., Emigh, J. and Ferris, L.K. (1999) *Masks: Faces of Culture*, New York: Harry N. Abrams, Inc.

Olesen, V. (1998) 'Feminisms and Models of Qualitative Research', in N.K. Denzin and Y.S. Lincoln (Eds), *The Landscape of Qualitative Research*, London: Sage Publications, pp. 300–332

Peirce, C.S. (1931) *Collected Papers. Vols I–VIII*, C. Hartshorne and P. Weiss (Eds), Cambridge, MA: Harvard University Press

Peters, T. and Waterman, R. (1982) *In Search of Excellence*, London: Harper & Row

Pollner, M. (1991) 'Left of Ethnomethodology: the Rise and Decline of Radical Reflexivity', *American Sociological Review*, Vol. 56: 370–380

Punch, M. (1998) 'Politics and Ethics in Qualitative Research', in N.K. Denzin and Y.S. Lincoln (Eds), *The Landscape of Qualitative Research: Theories and Issues*, London: Sage Publications, pp. 156–184

Reason, P. (1998a) 'Political, Epistemological, Ecological and Spiritual Dimensions of Participation', *Studies in Cultures, Organizations and Societies*, 4: 147–167

Reason, P. (1998b) 'Three Approaches to Participative Inquiry', in N.K. Denzin and Y.S. Lincoln (Eds), *Strategies of Qualitative Research*, London: Sage Publications, pp. 261–291

Reason, P. (2001) 'Learning and Change Through Action Research', in J. Henry (Ed.) *Creative Management* (Second edition), London: Sage Publications, pp. 182–194

Reason, P. (2006) 'Choice and Quality in Action Research Practice', *Journal of Management Inquiry*, Vol. 15, No. 2: 187–203

Reason, P. and Bradbury, H. (Eds) (2001) *Handbook of Action Research*, London: Sage Publications

Reason, P. and Heron, J. (1986) 'Research With People: the Paradigm of Co-operative Experiential Inquiry', *Person-Centred Review*, Vol. 1, No. 14: 456–476

Reason, P. and Rowan, J. (1981) 'Issues of Validity in New Paradigm Research', in P. Reason (Ed.) *Human Inquiry in Action – Developments in New Paradigm Research*, London: Sage Publications, pp. 239–250

Reed, B. (2001) *An Exploration of Role*, London: Grubb Institute

Reich, W. (1945) *Character Analysis*, New York: Orgone Institute Press

Richardson, L. (2002) 'Poetic Representation of Interviews', in J.F. Gubrium and J.A. Holstein (Eds), *Handbook of Interview Research: Context and Method*, Thousand Oaks, CA: Sage Publications, pp. 877–892

Riessman, C.K. (1993) *Narrative Analysis*, London: Sage Publications

Riley, R. and Manias, E. (2003) 'Snap-shots of live theatre: the use of photography to research governance in operating room nursing', *Nursing Inquiry*, Vol. 10, Issue 2, 81–90

Rippin, A. (2006) 'Refusing the Therapeutic: Marion Milner and Me', *Culture and Organization*, Vol. 12, No. 1: 25–36

Roberts, J. (1996) 'Management Education and the Limits of Technical Rationality: the Conditions and Consequences of Management Practice', in R. French and C. Grey (Eds), *Rethinking Management Education*, London: Sage Publications, pp. 54–75

Rogers, N. (2001) 'Person-Centred Expressive Arts Therapy: a Path to Wholeness', in J.A. Rubin (Ed.) *Approaches to Art Therapy – Theory and Technique*, New York: Brunner-Routledge, pp. 163–177

Rutter, K.A. (2003) 'From Measuring Clouds to Active Listening', *Management Learning*, Vol. 34, No. 4: 465–480

Sadler-Smith, E. (2004) 'Cognitive Style and the Management of Small and Medium-Sized Enterprises', *Organization Studies*, Vol. 25, No. 2: 155–181

Saunders (2003) 'On Flying, Writing Poetry and Doing Educational Research', *British Educational Research Journal*, Vol. 29, No 2: 175–187

Saunders, L. (2006) '"Something Made in Language": the Poet's Gift?', *Management Decision*, Vol. 44, No. 4: 504–511

Saussure, F. de (1966) *Course in General Linguistics*, Wade Baskin (Trans.), New York: McGraw-Hill

Schein, E.F. (1985) *Organizational Culture and Leadership*, San Francisco, CA: Jossey-Bass

Schein, E.H. (1992) *Organizational Culture and Leadership* (Second edition), San Francisco, CA: Jossey-Bass

Schein, E.H. (1993) 'On Dialogue, Culture, and Organizational Learning', *Organizational Dynamics*, Vol. 22: 40–51

Schön, D.A. (1987) *Educating the Reflective Practitioner*, San Francisco, CA: Jossey-Bass

Schreyögg, G. and Höpfl, H. (2004) 'Theatre and Organization: Editorial Introduction', *Organization Studies*, Vol. 25, No. 5: 691–704

Shotter, J. and Cunliffe, A.L. (2002) 'Managers as Practical Authors: Everyday Conversations for Action', in D. Holman and R. Thorpe (Eds), *The Manager as Practical Author*, London: Sage Publications

Simpson, P., French, R. and Harvey, C. (2002) 'Leadership and Negative Capability', *Human Relations*, Vol. 55, No. 10: 1209–1226

Sorell, W. (1973) *The Other Face: the Mask in the Arts*, London: Thames and Hudson

Stacey, R.D. (2003) *Strategic Management and Organizational Dynamics*, London: Prentice Hall

Stiles, D.R. (2004) 'Pictorial Representation', in C. Cassell and G. Symon (Eds), *Essential Guide to Qualitative Methods in Organizational Research*, London: Sage Publications, pp. 127–139

Strati, A. (1999) *Organization and Aesthetics*, London: Sage Publications

Tagore, R. (1912) *Gitanjali*, New Delhi: Full Circle Publishing Ltd. (New Edition 2004)

Taylor, S.S. (2002) 'Overcoming Aesthetic Muteness: Researching Organizational Members' Aesthetic Experience', *Human Relations*, Vol. 55, No. 7: 821–840

Torbert, W.R. (2001) 'The Practice of Action Inquiry', in P. Reason and H. Bradbury (Eds), *Handbook of Action Research: Participatory Inquiry and Practice*, Thousand Oaks, CA: Sage Publications, pp. 250–260

Vince, R. (1995) 'Working With Emotions in the Change Process: Using Drawings for Team Diagnosis and Development', *Organisations and People*, Vol. 2, No. 1: 11–17

Vince, R. and Broussine, M. (1996) 'Paradox, Defense and Attachment: Accessing and Working With Emotions and Relations Underlying Organisational Change', *Organization Studies*, Vol. 17, No. 1: 1–21

Von Krogh, G., Ichijo, K. and Nonaka, J. (2000) *Enabling Knowledge Creation*, New York: Oxford University Press

Watkins, C. (2006) 'Boundaries, Boundary Work and the Art of Management and Organisation Conferences: New Lines of Knowing', *Culture and Organization*, Vol. 12, No. 1: 3–10

Watkins, C., King, I. and Linstead, S. (2006) 'Introduction: Art of Management and Organization Conference Series', *Culture and Organization*, Vol. 12, No. 1: 1–2

Watkins, K.E. and Golembiewski, R.T. (1995) 'Rethinking Organization Development for the Learning Organization', *International Journal of Organizational Analysis*, Vol. 3, No. 1: 86–101

Weick, C.W. (2003) 'Out of Context: Using Metaphor to Encourage Creative Thinking in Strategic Management Courses', *Journal of Management Education*, Vol. 27, No. 3: 323–343

Weick, K.E. (1979) *The Social Psychology of Organizing*, Reading, MA: Addison-Wesley

Weick, K.E. and Browning, L. (1986) 'Argument and Narration in Organizational Communication', *Journal of Management*, Vol. 12, No. 2: 243–259

Weick, K.E. (1979) *The Social Psychology of Organizing*, Reading, MA: Addison-Wesley

Wheatley, M.J. (2002) *Turning to One Another: Simple Conversations to Restore Hope to the Future*, San Francisco, CA: Berrett-Koehler

Whyte, D. (1994) *The Heart Aroused: Poetry and the Preservation of the Soul in Corporate America*, New York: Doubleday

Wilson, N.C. and Stokes, D. (2005) 'Managing Creativity and Innovation – the Challenge For Cultural Entrepreneurs', *Journal of Small Business and Enterprise Development*, Vol. 12, No. 3: 366–378

Windle, R. (Ed.) (1994) *The Poetry of Business Life*, San Francisco, CA: Berrett-Koehler

Windle, R. (2006) 'Poetry and the business life', *Management Decision*, Vol. 44, No. 4: 457–463

Zuboff, S. (1988) *In the Age of the Smart Machine*, New York: Basic Books

INDEX